P9-CRZ-674

A TERRIBLE BEAUTY

A TERRIBLE BEAUTY

*Conversions in Prayer, Politics
and Imagination*

James Carroll

NEWMAN PRESS
New York/Paramus/Toronto

ACKNOWLEDGMENTS

Lyrics to *Miss American Pie* by Don Maclean, copyright ©
1971, 1972 by Mayday Music, Inc. and Yahweh Tunes,
Inc. All rights administered by Unart Music Corporation,
New York, N.Y. Used with permission.

The quotation from Leon Bloy's *Pilgrim of the Absolute* is
reprinted by permission of Pantheon Books, a division of
Random House Inc., copyright 1947.

Library of Congress
Catalog Card Number: 72-97400

ISBN 0-8091-0182-3

Published by Newman Press
Editorial Office: 1865 Broadway, N.Y., N.Y. 10023
Business Office: 400 Sette Drive, Paramus, N.J. 07652

Printed and bound in the
United States of America

Contents

I

COLLISIONS,
COLLAPSES,   CONVERSIONS
AND OTHER DROPS OF GOD'S REIGN

II

AT HOME IN EXILE:
POLITICS, POETRY, PRAYER

III

A TALE

. . . all changed,
changed utterly.
A terrible beauty is born.
W. B. Yeats.

An acknowledgment: I would like to thank Mary Ryan for her generous help in preparing this manuscript. Not to mention her friendship.

For
John Kirvan

I

Collisions, Collapses, Conversions and Other Drops of God's Reign

1
A Conversion to Gentleness

Was it fate or only the crowded subway that brought us together? She was a lovely young woman. Too lovely to stand so close and still be strangers. I tried, since I am Irish, not to look her in the eyes. I read the transit ads. I studied the maps of subway stops. I watched the tunnel light bulbs flashing by. Everytime I snuck my glance toward hers she was looking at me. Her eyes were very big, but not so deep. They flashed with the young, unknowing innocence to which most of us always run when we are frightened.

Finally, I stopped slipping my stare off hers. I looked her full in the face. She was still looking full at me. My blood was rushing. This could be it, I thought, capital letters and all.

The train jolted us against each other. I shifted my balance. She smiled. I nodded, as if from

3

Harvard. And then, finally, surprisingly, huski-
ly and at long last, she spoke. She spoke to *me*.
She said, "Are you a Christian?"

"Huh?" I said, stunned.

"Are you a Christian?" she asked again.
Since my fantasies are dreadfully predictable, I
had expected her to say "I love you" or "I want
your body" or "Come home with me." I never
thought she'd ask if I was a Christian.

And so, without planning it or being careful,
I answered her with the kind of spontaneous
and immediate simplicity that is peculiar to the
truth. I said, "No, I am not." My ancestors
would have called it denying the faith. They
would have died first. But they'd have understood, since they were people too, what the
dread moment of truthfulness is like. "No, I am
not," I said. Though I am a Catholic. And
though *by profession* or lack of it I *am* a religious man. Yet there I was saying: "*No,* I am
not a Christian." It was not so much that *I
knew not the man.* It was that I knew not myself. When I reached quickly to my own core I
was surprised.

I said, "No, I'm not." And with equal immediacy, spontaneity and truthfulness, the lovely
young woman looked away from me, feeling
noble and let down. I knew she was a Jesus-per-
son, a Jesus-freak, as we say. The definitions

with which she had been afflicted made it necessary that from the moment of my denial we
would be strangers, and we would be forever or
until I converted to the *one way*. She looked
away from me, and I wanted to grab her
shoulder and say, "Hey you, I will never
convert—*that* way. I will never surrender denial
or doubt or my dread ability to betray the
words I use and the people I love." Now, in
remembering it, I remind myself of Peter, who
would have screamed at Jesus on Pilate's bal-
cony: "Lord, goddammit, don't you turn from
me!" but for the fact that Jesus turned *toward*
him.

The times have made us strangers to ourselves. We have turned out so unlike what we
expected. So much in us and out of us has
changed. The words we use, even familiar ones
like *Christian, Catholic, religious* and *believer,*
have vague meanings that surprise us continually. As when we cannot use them of ourselves.
And so I said, "No. I am no Christian." Not in
that young woman's way. Not in my parents'
way. Not in the bishops' way. In whose way
then? Am I Christian in my own way? What is
that like? And what has it to do with the carpenter Christ? And with the Church? How do
we use the old words of ourselves while telling
the truth? We must approach the fragile lan-

guage of belief with care, else at our touch it crumbles into the clichés which kill us and, worse, make us boring.

"Are you a Christian?" Hell, I don't know. I do know I am a changed man and I am in search of words with which to speak of the change I carry in myself. I am change-made-flesh and I am looking for a way to tell you about it.

One of the old words we used to use—though never of ourselves—was a word about change. A word *of* change. A word whose business it was to make sense of radical change. And to praise it. The word of which I'm thinking is *conversion*. In Greek, *metanoia*—moving beyond. In good old Anglo-Saxon English, *turned around*. Though in the innocence of our arrogance the born believers of us thought we would be *converted* only at the peril of our souls, we have, in the good days of growing-up-chaos, been *turned around*. Fundamentally. Deeply. Radically. For the first time in our lives we claim the word *conversion* as our own. We have moved beyond *ourselves*!

How do you make sense of the change you have experienced? Remembering where you come from, how do you account for where you are? More has been going on than your growing up or growing old. More even than your loss of faith or your slipping into religious indifference. More than Vatican II or liturgical renewal or the peace movement or your first arrest. You have not only been changed. You have been *converted*. Or I have. Perhaps you should speak for yourself. Speaking for me, the *only* way I make any sense at all to myself now is as a *converted* man. That is what these pages are about.

"Are you a Christian?" I don't know. But I *am* a convert. That will have to be enough for now.

It is. But *convert* . . . to what?

To gentleness, perhaps.

I think of Elias and I say: "Elias, walk with me through these days and their dangers. It will be as nothing compared to your desert and your cave." I recognize in the figure of this old prophet the face of my own journey. Change? Conversion? Belief in God? Prayerfulness? He speaks to me of all these words with old Hebrew clarity. When you ask the haunting question "Are you a Christian?" the answer comes: "First I am a Jew." First I am Elias. This is my story.

Oh, I was an ever-righteous prophet. And tough. Armed with the Word of God, which told me I was right. It is marvelous being the messenger of the more than human. Licensed to pray, I went from idol to idol, smashing. And then, having grown in wisdom and grace, I went from idol-smasher to idol-smasher, smashing them. There is no pleasure to compare with being the first in fashion to know that the fashion is about to change. That's what a prophet is. I loved it.

Until the fashions smashed me. It is the feeling of that child who went from sand castle to sand castle, kicking away, destroying, leveling, grinding down, wiping out, all in the name, while laughing, of freedom. His own, mainly. When, after a long day's kicking down castles, he went home to his house on the dunes, it had been kicked down by someone else. Someone bigger whom he did not know. Or, in his frenzied power, had he kicked it down himself? His house, it turned out, was built on sand. Out of sand. That's the feeling I'm talking about.

After a hard day's challenging in the name of justice, I returned home for solace only to be challenged. Since I have been busy kicking the pins out of the world, why am I surprised that the world is falling away from me? While I smashed all those idols, the world was smashing me. Jezebel. Ahab. Mother. Father. Yahweh. Yesterday. "I am the last prophet left and they want to kill me." I'm leaving. Goodbye. Let me the hell out of here. *That* feeling.

And so the desert. Forty days. Forty nights. Without food. I only mention it because I was hungry. I lost more than weight. I lost glib speech. All the pretty words stopped protecting me from hunger. So I stopped using them. Or they stopped using me. You with your book— try silence. Try the mind-hunger which will not or cannot find the word which satisfies. Which speaks the truth. Which says what one means. Forty days of silence. Forty years. Forty million separate headaches. Go hungry once. And alone. I lost weight, glib speech and what we thought was friendship. We smashed not only idols but each other. "I am the last one left. And they want to kill me!"

And so collapse. I could not run any further. I had been running through all those headaches, all that silence, all that heat, all that hunger, all that loneliness. I quenched my thirst with tears and so learned to love my sorrows. But even weeping was taken finally. I was left without memory or expectation, without anger or re- morse. I was without bread in all its variety. I fell over. I went under. I stopped. I went to sleep, in the sand, in the shade, by the tree that killed me with its upright strength. I never knew I was such a weak man. I never knew death had hid in me all those years, waiting for its chance. Which came then, disguised as weariness. I curled up—to rest, I would have said, as I prepared to die.

And so the angel. I would have settled for a man. A friend. A woman. A lover. But it was an angel. I don't know what else to call it. Survival-made-flesh. I survived my own wish to die. I lived when there was nothing left. Out of hunger, silence, loneliness and sleep, there was fashioned a dream of bread, words of truth and friendship. It was the angel. I don't know what else to call it. A fellow from God. Who touched me. Who fed me. Who spoke kindly to me. Who turned me. Who changed me. If you had been there you would not have seen him. But you'd have seen me, getting up and going again, by damn. Alive, yessir. By damn hello! And going again. Alive. Alive. Oh. You'd have seen no angel. But you'd have seen me. Up. By damn. And leaping. Desert or no! Death or no!

And so Horeb. Mountain of God. High. After every desert there's a mountain. And you know what? The mountain can be worse. All that rock, immutable, unchanging, eternal, beyond the influence of little ones like us. There is no absence of the Lord like his presence. There is no loneliness like a friend who trusts you *after* your betrayal. There is no crime like justice. Be not just to me. Spare me the mountain. Spare me such permanence. When the world was what I wanted, I knew terror. I am not God. I am barely myself.

And so the cave. I went into hiding toward the end of my story. I mean *hiding*. I knew God would get me. I did not think it would take him so long. He came in the violent earthquake, and so I went deeper into the cave. He thought to scare me out and he scared me in. I screamed out at him, "I am the last one left and they want to kill me."

But the Lord Yahweh, who has never been a coward, did not know what that is like. And so he came to me again, but in a violent fire. Which drove me further than ever into the black, into the cavern of my hiding. I screamed out at him, desperate to be understood, "I am the only one left and they want to kill me!" I'm sure he thought I was paranoid or dramatic or exaggerating. But it was the *feeling* I had. I couldn't help it. I knew he'd never understand. By then I was so deep into the cave of Horeb that there was no light anywhere. I could hear my breathing in its quick struggle for air. I thought of myself choking and knew that when men go too deeply into caves they die. As a boy I once crawled into a tunnel and got stuck. My older brother saved me, though he was not a prophet. Certainly no angel. He was gone when I needed him again. I needed air. My breathing became violent, panicked, short. And then, surely, I would have died, finally, for all, but for the gentle breeze that came like light into the black cave. I breathed. I breathed again. I breathed easy. And I said to God, for surely it was he: "I am the last one left and they want to kill me." And oh what a cry I had. Shaking. Breathing, but barely.

But God, the Lord Yahweh, himself tender in the breeze, said only, "Get up, go to town and tell them what you learned." Which I did. Which I am doing. From the conflict and the collapse and the desert and the angel and the mountain and the cave and the easy breeze I learned *gentleness*. With myself. With my idols, which need smashing and loving both. With my weakness, with needs embrace as well as bracing. With you and your ways which are not mine. Nor ever will be. I learned gentleness with my names, both of them. They are *Elias* and *James*. We are converts. Pleased to meet you.

We are all learning. But what? We are learning from our failed renewals and peace movements and block unions and discussion groups and lost elections that the world is not what we want it to be. Our deserts refuse to be a garden. Our mountains won't move. Our caves are dark as any loneliness. Yet here we are alive and looking still for love. Yet here we are knowing how to laugh. Yet here we are telling each other what we have learned.

We have learned a lot, though we find it hard to say exactly how. We remember Bobby Kennedy saying with Shaw: "Some people see things as they are and ask 'Why?' I see what never was and ask 'Why not?' " And we want to say: What about the other possibility, which is to see what is and ask of *that*: "Why not?" Our poignant dissatisfaction with what is, whether politically or religiously, is a dissatisfaction, finally, with ourselves. We are harsh with what is and hard on it because we are harsh with ourselves and hard on everything. We are hung between bleak reality and lovely dreams, but ever deprived of simple waking joys. We need to be converted to *gentleness*, with ourselves and with each other. It is a conversion that occurs *through* gentleness.

To get up from our desert sleep is to admit weariness and claim cowardice as our own. What have we learned? We have learned we are no heroes. We are the people who do not go to jail for our convictions. We are the people who make a peace with war and let someone else worry about all those bombs. We are the people who forget and eat lettuce, who laugh at racist jokes, who break promises all the time. We talk a lot about faithfulness and justice and peace because we live so far from all of it. We are—how did we used to put it?—sinners. *Confiteor Deo.*

It is not a bad place to begin—that knowledge. If I write with any consolation, it is the specific and certain knowledge that you are with me in this. We are sinners together. And so we say: "Remember, Mac, you are dust. You are going back to dust." To dirt. To ash. To earth. To a cave.

If there is good news here—and there may not be, though we always look for it—it is that the earth, the ash, the dirt, the dust is all right. A fruitful place to be. To discover one's own sin and to *survive the discovery*—that is called *conversion.* I am no hero. I am a sinner. I am also still alive. You are still with me. Perhaps, maybe, I am still interesting to you, to someone.

When I am in my cave, will you come after me? Yes, you will. You have. You are doing it now. Forgive me if your terrible earthquake drives me farther into darkness. I do not need your lectures. I do not need your righteous indignation. Don't come at me with whips. I will not turn your tables over. We have been harsh on each other, haven't we? All that guilt we threw around. Why, it got so I felt guilty for feeling guilty. I *know* I am responsible for the world, for all creation, for the order of the cosmos. Don't beat me with it. I can hardly handle the small garden out behind the house. You remind me of my alarm clock screaming at me to get up from bed. *I will not get up until the screaming stops.* Go elsewhere with your earthquakes.

The caves into which we have crawled are invincible, like the base of Thunder Mountain, part Pentagon, part catacomb, part James Bond hideout, part electric blanket over one's head. We will not come out until the screaming stops. We hide here with our vast consumption, buying something new whenever we get worried. We buy things, clothes, travels, experiences, religious and otherwise. We buy friendship and quiet and speed and sexual identity. My car is redder than your car. We are so glad we have the money, but we wonder now and then why the penniless seem not to envy us. Who are the victims anymore? The trouble with this cave, though it is safe and soft, is it's too damn dark.

Who will come after me? Who will pursue me? Who will turn me out? Around? Inside myself? Will you? Don't chase me with your fire. I do not need a scorching. I do not want napalm on *my* head. I was against the war. I was against the fire. What could *I* do? You think I like impotence? You think this feeling of no power over anything that matters is a favorite of mine? Don't turn your anger on me or I'll turn mine on you! Damn right, by God! I have anger that hasn't been invented yet. I have fire of my own. I could destroy the world. We are right to be afraid.

I can hide from everything except what frightens me most—my fear. To discover one's fear and survive the discovery—*that* is called conversion. I am afraid of nothing, except what moves and what doesn't move. I am afraid of you. I am afraid of myself. Show me the cave deep enough for such hiding as *that*.

Once you discover your sin and once you discover your fear, something else happens that surpasses language. I have been calling it survival. I have been calling it conversion. Metanoia. Turning around. Elias calls it a gentle breeze.

When you have been crawling as fast as you can go, as deep into the Thunder Mountain Pentagon-catacomb as your knees will take you, something sometimes happens, as it has to us. A faint wind. A gentle aroma. Not much. But enough to make you stop. Enough to make your knees remember prayer. Your hunger remembers bread. Enough to turn you around.

God keeps doing it. His breezes breathe. We are coming out. We are returning to the people. I am returning to you. No hero, I drag my cave with me. My sin survives all conversions. The Pentagon clings to its defensiveness. But still I return, having been turned. I meet you on the way. We are learning and we need to tell each other what. Who.

And so you say to me, "Are you a Christian?" And I say, "I am a convert." But you, seeing me in my cave still, persist, "Are you a Christian?"

I reach deep down, past the desert sleep, the cowardice, the sin, the false humility, and I come up with a gentle breeze which says for me simply, "Yes." The breeze whispers then in my ear alone, "The holy words you use of yourself are how you become who you already are." We laugh.

2
The Conversion of Collapse

"Well, watchman, what of the night?"
"You mean, you're the only one who hasn't heard?"
"Heard what?"
"About the night . . . how it turned . . . this morning . . . into day."

That is a true story. Night did that once. In fact, night did it yesterday. We were talking about *conversion*. Metanoia. Turning around, moving beyond. Radical change. Do you remember? You were saying things are different. You are different. We were looking together for ways to explain it ourselves, this feeling. This change. This conversion.

And along comes night. Turning into day. Just yesterday. Just now. Perhaps we should stop talking and listen.

Night, day and the earth's turning are telling us a story. It is the story of your typical affluent liberal with good looks. His name is Job. It is not the story, as you are thinking, of suffering. It is the story of how one man's night turned into day, once in the land of Uz.

It was not easy. Now you and I know that your typical affluent liberal with good looks is in for trouble. Anybody who's had it good will have it bad—the times and the Irish need to fail have always told us it is so.

It is especially so now when the bill has come due for the Vietnam War, which is our own metaphor for murdered Cain and for the tower of lies. When a bill like this falls due, someone has to pay it and keep paying. And so we do. In our cities, as wealth turns to ashen air. In our lovely countryside, as earth turns to concrete. In our families, as children leave quietly. In our schools, as crimes replace prankishness and drug addiction replaces bubble gum. There is an Old Testament vengeance in the air. Whose story is this? Which of us is not Job?

If we are quiet perhaps we can find out what's coming. Let's listen to God plotting with his devil. It is our bug in heaven. Quiet.

"Well, devil, where have you been?"
"Oh . . . around the earth. Roaming

about."

"Did you notice my servant Job. A terrific fellow. Pious too."

"Yes. But not for nothing. Look at all you've given him. Take it all away and he'll curse your face."

"Oh yeah? Want to bet?"

"You're on."

"O.K. Let's get him."

And so they do. And that's the beginning of the long dark night of Job. Think of your worst day, ever. That was years for him. Floods, wars, muggers, too much drink, kids ruined by freaky friends. Job lost his plow, his ox, his camel, his credit rating, his club. He lost his job. He tore his gown; he shaved his head. He said, "Naked I came. Naked I go." It was a bad night, and though in all this misfortune Job offered no insult to God, God and the devil were not through yet. Job got ulcers. His house fell down on all his children, killing them. And finally his wife left him to his dung heap. Her last words invited him to curse God and die. He said nothing. When his preacher-friends came with their good news he cursed his birthday. It was that kind of night. Ruins all around. There was nothing for him to do but get to know himself real well.

When you have lost everything, including

meaning, health and affection for God, something happens. What happened to Job was this —*conversion.* Turning point. Discovery. He made the discovery that his *life,* his *being,* depended on no possession, no relationship, no position, no virtue. Depended on nothing. Literally on no-thing. Job survived the loss of everything, including meaning, belief and good manners. Not only that. When he saw himself stripped clean, naked, alone, exposed, vulnerable, collapsed, he liked what he saw. He liked *himself.* He was not nearly so bad as all those salesmen had been telling him. He saw himself in God's eyes and liked it. "Having seen you with my own eyes," he said to God and therefore to himself, "I take back all my curses." You are good. And I guess I am too. My God, is this grace? Is this survival with style? Job's two difficult words for happiness are *radical poverty.* When you are down to nothing you are ready to begin. Naked you came—and you weren't so bad at the start, you know. Naked you go. Good. A man. Amen. Alle—as we say in the trade—luia.

It is the discovery which waits to be made by us. Put most simply, we need to be converts from consumerism. Socially we need to be converted from capitalism. Consumerism is the root not only of war and of ecological disaster.

It is how we hide from our real selves and from each other. The souring of affluence, which is most clearly represented by the vast unhappiness of affluent children, is a moment of grace. If the objects of your purchase, whether things, travel or experiences, leave you slightly bored, perhaps you are getting ready to learn what Job learned. It will not be easy.

These are what Adam Smith calls "the last days of cowboy capitalism." One of the ways in which we are changed is this: we *do not* believe that what is good for General Motors is good for the world or even for us. With Pope Paul VI we are more likely to suspect that what is good for America's corporate power is disastrous for the rest of us. (See *Progressio Populorum.*) Job's goal, like that of any corporation executive, was to maximize profit. When his profits were ripped away from him, he screamed for a while and then began to live. The profits of our economic systems are being taken from us. Affluence is going sour. And maybe just in time. We are in the midst of a critical *conversion,* economically, socially, personally, religiously.

We are learning that productivity alone is no source of happiness. It is not enough to say we are what we do. Notwithstanding electoral pieties, the work ethic does not work. We may long for the days when work was everything, but deeper than our own voting, we have been changed. We want to know. What happens when we get old? When we can't work? When we can't produce? When we are useless? Do they shoot us? Do they give us pills to keep us quiet? Do they send us somewhere nice? Will they do to us what we have done to our parents? God help us, who are *they* but our children?

Kurt Vonnegeut suggests that the key problem of our age is how to love people who are of no use. How do we love what is useless in ourselves? How do we love ourselves when *we* are of no use? We all run around from base to base, frenzied, busy, scheduled to the teeth, proving to each other how *useful* we are. We are keeping the man with the little black pills away.

Me, for example. I bust my ass. I get up at dawn and quite literally I run around Boston Common by the marble vestiges of revolution. I shower. I do my teeth—with *dental floss*, for God's sake. I read two papers. Wash the dishes. Get in my prayers. And *then*, after two hours of semi-conscious busy-ness, I go to *work*. I am so fevered with this Nixonitis that even in my leisure I am Protestant and productive. Quality of life *as task*. Doing nothing becomes a way of working. Buy stock in recreation. Buy. Buy. Buy.

Think of fishing. In America, Brother David

says, we are not allowed to do nothing (since *we are what we do*). We are allowed only to go fishing. And what is fishing? Fishing is sitting by water with a pole with some string tied to it and hoping that the fish will leave the string alone. When a fish bites, it messes the whole thing up because you have to come out of your reverie and sit up and pull it in and touch it with your bare hands and put it in your wicker basket when you'd rather throw it back in the water. If you threw the fish back in the water you couldn't prove you'd spent the day "doing something useful." Fishing is *doing nothing all the day* with a pole between your legs. If you didn't have the pole your family would think you were depressed, crying for help by doing nothing, contemplating suicide maybe. Why else would you be sitting by the river all day long? If you didn't have the pole some people would think you were a Democrat on welfare. If you didn't have the pole, they'd take you away eventually. Doing nothing is not allowed. We do not love what is useless in time or in ourselves.

In secret each of us suspects that we are in deep and basic ways *profoundly useless*. The suspicion terrifies. So we gather around our neighborhood Jobs and jeer. We attack the uselessness in others, whether the sick or the old or the dirt poor, because we fear it so in ourselves.

But the story of Job proclaims the good news that such fear is unnecessary—not because we are ultimately useful, but because our uselessness is profoundly lovable and dignified. We can dare *to go fishing without a pole* because doing nothing is an act of love and dignity. Our honor depends on no status, on no output, on no "earning"; we are honorable because we are. When Job loses his job, so to speak, he begins to live. He begins to live close to the bone of existence.

At that bone several things become clear. Loneliness dissolves in the discovery that *all people* are useless in precisely the way that in secret we know ourselves to be. What we have been hiding from in our possessiveness is what joins us to others. We can come out of hiding when we discover close to the bone the one *life of being* we share with all people. We can stop our mad pursuit of riches and power. We can stop the deadly collecting of things, experiences and people that keeps us in debt and bored to tears. We are not nearly so bad, so unworthy, so ugly as all those salesmen keep telling us. When they say that we are useless, hoping to stir us in our deepest fear, we can reply, "Yes. As is art and poetry and laughter and everything lovely. In our uselessness we are human." Having seen *ourselves useless and poor* with our own eyes we can take back all our curses.

Belief is the struggle to see yourself the way that God would if he had eyes. God sees from the point of view of the *radically poor*. God is radical poverty itself. His worth depends on nothing, on no thing, no task, no relationship, no job, no Job. God is. Period. *Ipsum Esse* (for those of us who won't believe what can't be said in Latin). God has nothing. God does nothing. God *is*. Period. "Sometimes I sits and thinks," the child said. "And sometimes I just sits." *That's* the idea of God that God has.

It sounds as if I am trying to speak for God. What arrogance! I am speaking, of course, for myself. I believe that it is precisely in my own radical poverty that I meet God. In my nearness to nothingness which philosophy calls being. In my uselessness. In my powerlessness. It is the lesson I learn from Job. It is the lesson I learn from my own experience.

The argument that we overheard between God and the devil is not carried on in heaven. It is carried on in me. In you, unless you're different. The argument comes in all words, packages and shapes. But God and the devil get it down to basics. Job's happiness depends on what he *has* and on what he *does*. No, Job's happiness springs from the fact that he *is*. It is the clash of points of view that translates in political and national terms into wars. If what you *have* and what you *do* protect you from unhappiness and from your fears, then you *must* collect possessions and you *must* work ninety hours a week and you must conquer other peoples and punish them for demanding a share in the resources you hoard. If you take the devil's side in the argument you *must* be a consuming social climber in your private life and a corporate capitalist in your public life. Conversion begins with the admission that we all have this constitutional tendency to take the devil's side.

Grace is the regular surprise that God takes our side. Usually his alliance with us involves the kind of stripping and destroying that we associate with Job. It is as important as it is difficult for us to go beyond (move beyond) our usual perception of Job as the pathetic victim to a new perception of Job as a fully liberated man. It is not that he loses his possessions and his relationships but that he is *converted* in the way he experiences them. When Job's story is told to the end he is not the devil's man. What he *has* and what he *does* are not the source of his happiness, but *gifts* that flow from the basic happiness of being loved by God out of nothing into being. *Gifts* belong to no one, but everyone is responsible to keep them gifts. It is not that "workfare" people give gifts to "welfare" people, but that all people share the *one gift* of life and earth. That current distinction is the heinous blasphemy that leads always to material possessiveness and often to the human possession which we call slavery.

God is the one who calls us continually out of slavery. We are being called now, by the chaos of our times and by the pressures of world revolution, out of *our* slaveries to possessions and to productivity. When we are converted to real faith we will not seek to buy salvation as if it were a split-level home; to earn it as if it were a five-figure income. We will cherish salvation as God's gift. We will delight in the knowledge that *nothing* we do or have is worth the gift of one day's life in Boston, much less eternity with God. Our political systems groan with the need for such conversion; when affluent liberals like ourselves leave our suburban Egypts, at last the world itself will be a freer place. Property, profits, and all human and natural resources will serve the one life of humanity and not the special interests of the wealthy.

Our personal lives groan with the need for such conversion; when we break our endless circle of achievement, restlessness and new achievement, we will discover each other. We buy our houses and our jobs and our successes with squandered inheritances. We will discover our loves, our friends, our dear selves when we can literally *do nothing together*. You can tell whether you love anyone by asking whether you *waste time* with anyone. If every moment of your life is useful and productive you may be admired by many, but you are alone. And you know it. It was the time the little prince *wasted* on his rose that made it precious to him. And so it is with us. The most precious gift I can give to you is my uselessness. If I give you *everything,* you are in my debt. If I give you the gift of *shared-nothing,* I love you. I give strangers my successes. My failures I save for my friends.

A conversion to relaxation. *Nothing doing,* as we say, all the day. "There is nothing to do," Rozack says, "nowhere to get. We need only stand still in the light." Our slaveries spring from what we're proving and to whom. With most of our energy we prove our *usefulness* and worth to each other and to ourselves. We are frustrated because in a basic way we know we are neither useful nor worthy. Death has a hold on us. Our belief in the God of Job offers a way out of such slavery. The God of Job is the one to whom we need prove nothing. We are utterly and dramatically useless to God. He needs nothing of us. What comes from such a God as that *must* come as gift. There are no deals. No purchases. No proofs needed. God is the one with whom we can relax. Waste time. When we are free enough we will waste eternity with him.

In the meantime we must make do with each other and with the gift of eternal moments now and then. Moments of pure joy, of love, of accidental laughter, of creativity. Moments when we say, "Ah—*that* is what I'm made for!" Moments of ecstasy, of being close to nothingness itself. Moments of grace.

It is those quick and fleeting times when we *glimpse* ourselves as we long to be that hold out the promise for us that happiness is possible. Indeed that we are happy now, perhaps. Just maybe. With our clinging slaveries and our compulsions and our productivity and our fear of stopping all this busy-ness. Even now, as I come to the end of this section, I think: *What will I do when I'm through?* I am not free enough yet to go fishing without a pole. To live without the symbols of achievement, to care *really* about those hungry ones who long for the bread I hoard.

But hoarded bread goes stale. And my protected comfort collapses in a world gone awry. And I cannot hide from my loneliness anymore. And I discover like Job the advantage to living in a time of peculiar chaos. It is this: I *know* I need to be converted. To be changed. To be turned around. To be moved beyond, as *met-*

anoia means. The knowledge of this need is a promise of its possibility. And a signal of its beginning to be fulfilled. I am like Job. So are we all. With our love of possessions and affluence and achievements and the relationships we have collected. We are like Job in our fear of being stripped and our anger when it happens. We are like him in our clenched fists raised to heaveṇ. But we are like him also in our ability to *see* God when he appears in our midst, disguised as truth or as hunger or as hope. And when we see God, believing like Job, we take back our curses. We fall silent. We imitate God and touch our own goodness carefully. We embrace our uselessness. We forgive our sin.

Though we resist this growth in freedom and cling to yesterday—yesterday always fools us by turning into tomorrow, night always into day—conversion, moving beyond, is possible because there is more here than us, though with our loud screaming one would think not.

But night turns into day.

And even screams have ways of turning into promises and glad shouts and finally laughter.

3
A Conversion to Connection

It was the judge in the trial of the Milwaukee Fourteen who did it for us; he wept. In the act of sentencing my Boston brother Tony Mullaney, he, as the *New York Review* reported, "choked on that good Irish name and fumbled among his black robes for a handkerchief. He wept for a few seconds, and then in a timorous voice resumed sentencing the monk who stood before him triumphantly, dressed in clerical black, his arms folded as if he were the executioner."

God knows for whom the court weeps. Probably, like all of us, for itself. And probably, for more.

One's response to the presence of a prophet seems always to begin in weeping. Partly because every prophet is part executioner and, when the times are bad, mercilessly so. We weep for fear because our world, we know, is about to be ripped from us. We weep also because a prophet before us always confronts us with the immense sadness we bear for the world by confronting us with the specific ways we make it worse. Which is why we keep our prophets at a distance, either by putting them in jail or on the cover of *Time*. The thing is to get the prophet out of our city so we can honor him. Or onto a cross so we can love him. (Is it only on the cross that we love a prophet or a Jew?)

I have been fortunate in my own unlucky way. The troublesome, fearful, executing, accusing faces who have prodded me to a *position* of radicalism, religious and political, have loved me also and enough to forgive me my ever so mannered, slightly mystic and dreadfully liberal *temperament*—which continues intact despite their assaults. (The useful distinction between position and temperament is in Martin Green's *Cities of Light and Sons of the Morning*.) Chief among my prophets have been my kid brother Dennis and Catholic resisters like Anne Walsh with whom I work at Boston University. They have both, on occasion, made me weep. And they have both taught me how to dance. I mention them because the prophets among us are the ones in whose presence we change. Dennis changed me by refusing to be drafted long ago when only cowards and world champions did that. I tried to talk him out of it; he talked me into the Vietnamese. Anne, with her own record of alleged burglaries and fasts, changed me by being *religiously* radical, showing me how to find Jesus in the mess of our days together in Boston.

We have been talking about change. About conversion. About moving beyond. Metanoia! About turning around. Though I only now use their names, I have been talking all along about Dennis and Anne. And some others. You have yours. You have your private prophets. The people who made you weep for fear and sadness. The people who insisted on looking at the world differently—and then insisted on sharing their eyes with you. I write as an act of thanksgiving for them. And, as always, in preparation for our next argument over eyesight.

It is important to know what has happened to us. The conversion that is occurring in our lives is the result of prophecy. The world itself has taken a prophetic stand toward us: ruthless, moralistic, unyielding. It says to us, in Auden's words, "Love each other or die!" Our Dennises and Annes and Tonys and Daniels and Philips all speak on the world's behalf with the world's words. Love each other or die. In the tough moment of the challenge a new unity occurs—it was new for me, at least. Suddenly and for a moment religion and radicalism are the same thing. Suddenly and for a moment I am ready *really* to leave everything and follow; I am ready to live totally for the future and some democratic utopia we call a kingdom; I am ready even to be a eunuch for its sake. Suddenly and for a moment I am free. I choose to love you and not to die.

But the moment, just as suddenly, passes. I am not loving you. I *am* dying. The trouble with the truth a prophet speaks is that it makes everything else a lie. Though I choose a *position* of radicalism, an unradical *temperament* has been chosen for me. I live somewhere between the truth and the lie. And though I am not proud of that, neither am I ashamed. During Lent's six week journey to Jerusalem, I am like Peter trying to block your path to death. Don't go, I am saying. Let us love each other and not die. I am confused when you reply, "Get behind me, Satan. We must love each other *and* die!" When that happens I never know what to say. I just tag along, trying to keep my mouth shut. It is dangerous to speak like a prophet when you lack the prophet's clarity. I am more like Peter than Paul. I am more like David than Nathan.

David and Nathan. An old story. An old testament. It is worth telling again since it is our
story. You be Nathan. Let me be David.

"Look," I says, "I am living in a fine house
of cedar while the ark of God dwells in a tent.
Aren't I terrific? It is not what you think, for
the Lord God who gave me fame as great as the
fame of the greatest on earth, who worked great
and terrible things on my behalf, he it is who
gave me this house. Indeed the Lord has spoken
and with his blessing my house will be forever
blessed."

But that Nathan, with his hard eyes, says to
me, "Look, David, why should you have a
cedar house when the Lord has a lousy tent?"

"If that's the way he wants it, who am I to
complain? Should I refuse his gifts? Let him
build his own house if he wants one. As for me,
I am but a simple and pious king."

After that I defeated the Philistines and won
the cold war with the Moabites. Everyone paid
me tribute. I collected power and big towns. I
won fame for myself, and wherever I went,
Yahweh gave me victory. For which, of course,
I was grateful. In addition I grew in wisdom
and in grace. Not only that, I married Uriah's
lovely young widow.

But that Nathan, with his hard eyes, comes
bearing tales of some injustice done in my king-

dom. Any injustice done in my kingdom, understand, will not go unpunished. Nevertheless,
that Nathan always makes me feel funny, somehow. He is a hard man to like. He is talking to
me:

"In the same town were two men, one rich,
the other poor. The rich man had flocks and
herds in great abundance; the poor man had
nothing but a ewe lamb, one only. A small one
he had bought. This he fed and it grew up with
him and his children, eating his bread, drinking
from his very cup, sleeping on his breast. It was
like a daughter to him, for he was a poor but
tender man.

"One day a traveler came to stay with the
rich man. And do you know what the rich man
did? Instead of taking one of his own large flock
or herd for food for his guest, he took the poor
man's lamb and killed it and served it cooked as
food. The rich man ate the poor man's love!"

Well my anger, let me tell you, flared up
against the man. "As Yahweh lives," I said to
Nathan, "the man who did this deserves to
die!"

And then that Nathan, with his hard eyes,
said to me, "You, David, are the man."

And I knew it was the truth. I understood. I
fumbled among my robes for a handkerchief. I
wept for a few seconds. But that Nathan stood

before me triumphantly, in his prophet's dress, his arms folded as if he were my executioner.

Then he said to me, "Thus Yahweh speaks, 'I will stir up evil for you out of your own cedar house. You work injustice in secret. I will work retribution in the full face of the sun.' "

I could think of nothing else to say to Nathan but: "I have sinned against the Lord Yahweh."

And he replied, "You sin against the poor. You sin against yourself."

It was the truth. I said, "I see." And then fell silent.

In the story of David's changed *seeing,* I am changed. Conversion occurs when one sees through the eyes of another. The prophet is the one who forces other eyes on us. I said before that you could be Nathan. I would be David. But we are both of them, both of us. How do the rich, the powerful, the easy of us see with the eyes of the poor on whose possessions we trample, of the hungry on whose last ewe lamb we feed? It is a matter of *seeing connections,* what we have been calling conversion. See the connection between yourself and the other. If you insist on living in a fine house of cedar, someone will always live in a mud-flat tent. It may be God. What then?

The history of these years has been a history

of our early outrage at the sins of the world. Do you remember the intensity of that first connection when you understood racism or when you saw the moral horror of Vietnam. Do you remember crying after Birmingham, after Memphis, after Attica, after Mylai: "By God, whoever is responsible for this should die"? Or words to that effect. Remember how we began the exorcism of our cities and governments and local boards, trying to find the devil, to cast him out, if not kill him? And along came Nathan, with his simple message that *we* are responsible. It is you! We have heard and we have seen the truth of that proclamation. For now we are fumbling still in our robes. Trying not to cry because we know that tears at this point, like guilt, are just another hiding place, another dodge. Surely when, as now, the truth is told about our consistent selfishness, we can see something more than our own weeping pain. How about *seeing* the pain of the brothers who died in the federal government's Hitler-like syphilis experiments?

Seeing! Conversion is a matter of *seeing*. Seeing connections. David sees his own connection with the social crimes of his kingdom. Suddenly, his lusts, his petty insecurities, his foibles, his cruelties all take on a new and darker color when their connections with the plight of another are made visible. We remember David as a poet, as an artist, as a lover, as a good king—all of which he was because of this conversion to the capacity for connecting. It is the conversion to imagination. Though David could not *see* exactly how what he did affected a peasant, he could *imagine* it. And so can we. So must we. To *imagine* how the use of our resources depletes someone else's—unless we develop that capacity personally and nationally, we all die. We must see connections or die. Justice is the ability to see connections and live by them.

And it has happened to us. The world, the very times, have been *Nathan* to us. Everything is connected to everything else—and we are learning that. Though we do not, most of us, see with the clarity of a prophet, we do see more and more with the prophet's instincts for connection. So we live trying to keep things together: poetry, prayer, politics, Chicanos, lettuce, Russia, abortion, priesthood, laughter. Today we—I—see connections as never before. At its most basic level, that is what change has done to us. We have learned from our several revolutions. Once we see one connection, everything is different. Mainly, *we* are different. We do not *see* as detached observers. We are not the glib critics who live without commitments, though we have been tempted by the lonely lux-

ury of that position. For the connections we discover extend in and through and with and
around *ourselves*. *We* are the ones! Who eat
scab lettuce. Who pay war taxes. Who suspect
blacks on city elevators. Who eat the last ewe
lamb of the poor man. *And we* are the ones who
are pressing for the reform of prisons, who expect accounting from authority, who are not
buying the latest fashions this year. *We* live between the truth and the lie. How Nathan deals
with *his* conscience and *his* connection with op-
pression—and surely he is connected, guilty, too
—is his business. We are David. We do not
claim prophecy. We do claim responsibility,
however. We are Nathans by *position,* perhaps.
By temperament we are Davids. We are embarrassed by our former arrogance. We know we
have sinned against each other. And against
ourselves. We see that *now*!

But we need a new Nathan who can remind
us that we have sinned against *God.* The connection we discover extends that far. Or that
close. One might even say, though it is silly,
that God's new name, as if he needs another
one, is Connection itself. (*Ipsum Connectare,*
for those who do not speak to God in English.)

We are making this huge effort to recover
transcendence, to preserve our ability to use
words of mystery, to say to the worlds beyond

without apology, "Hello, how are you today?" We are trying still to speak of God. Such are the connections we see that this is not something separate. This is not a new thing or a different responsibility.

These days it is easier to see our connection with the poor man than it is to see our connection with God. *That* is the key result of the conversion of which we speak, and it is *exactly* as it should be. "Deal with your brother before you deal with me." But "deal with me." We cannot do either without both. If our changed vision does not include God in its range of focus, we see *nothing* as it really is. If we are not religious, I dare to claim, we are not nearly alive enough. If we are not "rhapsodically afire," to use Rozack's description of faith, we are nearly burnt out. We are cold and in the dark.

When we are alive to the unities of our existence with each other we are alive to God. There is *One Life* in which we all share and to which belief speaks as if it were a father. The One Life we share overcomes death in all its forms. The prophet who faces us with our sin faces us also with the good news that no sin of ours can break the connection, finally, which holds us in being and union with everything that is. We cannot live alive to the power of God's love until, having *seen* our sin, we *see* that we cannot obliterate that power.

When I was David, having seen, I said to Nathan, "I have sinned against Yahweh." Then Nathan said to me, "Yahweh, for his part, forgives your sin; you are not to die."

Oh, God, did you hear that? *Forgives my sin! I am not to die!* I want to believe that so much that I actually *look* for Nathans to say it to me. And they do. My Dennises and Annes. Especially the ones whose last lamb I eat. Forgiveness is possible between us because there is more to our connection than either of us brings to it. There is bigness and deepness and a gentleness that always surprises. There is grace. We can forgive each other everything because we live always in the embrace of a love which is more than human.

Nathan comes to us with *two* words. He says of sin, "*You* are the one!" And we see and we are about to go away with our weeping and our guilt. And then he says, this time of forgiveness, "*God* is the one!" And we become the *other* David, the poet, the singer, the sayer of psalms. The great lover. The free one afire.

It is the conversion for which we have been waiting. Sin into, as we say in Latin, salvation. Remorse into rhapsody afire. Guilt into conviction. It is not that our selfishness, our moral failure, is removed, denied or condoned. But

that God is not subject to it, and therefore neither are we. We *can* change. We *can* end exploi-
tation and racism and systemic oppressions and
petty selfishness. We *can* love each other, and
live. Judgment, stern, fearful, difficult, makes
healing possible. We might hate our Nathans
when they come to us executioner-like, but we
can love them too. They do not kill us after all,
but call us to life. In addition to being a prophet, remember, Nathan is a man who hides from
a sin of his own, until he hears a word of forgiveness from you.

And so, having choked and fumbled in our
robes and wept, we are prepared now, with the
new David, to dance. We can dance before the
ark. We can unfold our arms and dance in the
court of law. We can dance before all our
judges, prophets, Nathans, and even before all
our victims, who are as partners to us now. For
we can dance before the Lord God himself.

4
A Conversion to Immediacy

I learn more from my failures than from my
successes. Yesterday I preached what would
have been a great sermon about how God is *really* present to his people. Great but for the fact
that, wherever God was during that sermon, *I*
was not present to the people. I was not present
even to myself. As I rambled on preaching, ser-
monizing, theologizing, the dread little voice
from over my shoulder kept whispering into my
third ear, "That isn't it at all. That isn't what
you mean at all." There is no lie to compare
with a failed sermon; as I beat the air with my
glib truth God may have been there, Jesus may
have been there, my seminary teacher may have
been there, some of the bored people may have
been there—but I wasn't. I was sitting on my
shoulder, shaking my head, embarrassed.

I think I know what went wrong. Unlike the

Jews, who always began by talking about themselves, I began by talking about God. What my
failed sermon taught me is this: our problem is
not that God is distant from us, but that we are
distant from ourselves. *That* must be our start-
ing point. It matters not at all if God is really
present to us unless we are too. In preaching, in
loving, in laughing, in dying.

Our common fear, as the airline ads reveal to
us, is that the best years of our lives are happening without us. Our disease is our dis-ease—that
we are observers, not participants. Those of us
in campus ministry used to describe ourselves as
the "marginal people." You could find us on
the edge of every riot, every meeting, whether
SDS or faculty, watching, looking, criticizing,
saying under our breath, "That isn't it at all.
That isn't what you mean at all." We sat on the
shoulders of everyone else. We called ourselves
"marginal" and tried to make a virtue of our
detachment, though we hated it and longed to
lose ourselves in the very middle of something
once. And then one day we discovered that everyone in the university feels this way; everyone
is marginal. Everyone is detached. Everyone experiences the university as someone else's issue,
someone else's place. And then one day we discovered that politicians and journalists and bureaucrats and policemen and bankers and exec-

utives all feel this way; everyone, everywhere is marginal. Marginal not just to the Vietnam war or to the political process but to themselves. It is not that God is banished from our lives but that we are.

How do we climb down from our own shoulders? How do we stop being leprechauns to ourselves? We are witty, bright, cynical and smart. But if we lack compassion for ourselves, how can we possibly have it for the crucified? We are highly critical, having learned to detect fraud and ruthlessly expose it. But what is criticism without commitment, if not cruelty?

It is as hard to be present to oneself and one's own world as it is to believe that *God* is really present to us and our world. And *that* is hard. Indeed the two struggles are one. When we speak seriously of God we are speaking chiefly of ourselves. When we say, as we have lately, that God is gone or distant or impersonalized or vague, we are also saying that lately we have been this grey shade of ourselves, wisping through our days with all the color and sub- stance of, say, smoke. What we need is to touch our flesh again *with* our flesh. To touch God's spirit *with* God's spirit as it lives in our breath- ing. We need the gutsy and slightly immoderate and unsophisticated gift of, say, presence. When I call your name, stand up and say "Present" or

"Here I am" or "*Adsum*" or, bloomingly, "Yes, yes, yes, yes!" Carroll! Carver! Carpenter! Christ!

Jesus! Where was he if not *here*! Not *there*! We are always putting God and everything important about ourselves (integrity, happiness, haircut) over *there*! Which is always across vast acres of time or space or accomplishment or schooling or churching or growing up. God is over *there,* in heaven. My happiness is over *there* in that brave new marriage. *There!* It would be such a great place to live. Gertrude Stein paid it a visit once, via Los Angeles, and sent back this report: "When I got there there was no *there* there." That's the trouble with *there.* We are always stuck with *here.* So . . . when I call your name, answer.

Jesus! He was God's reply to the perennial human effort to banish significance and sanctity to the vanishing island we are calling *there.* Jesus was God's Word that he is *here,* not *there*! If God has gone to all that trouble to get here, he wants us to get here too. If he can do it, we can.

How do we climb down from our own shoulders, from *there* to *here*? Ask someone who's done it. Say, for example, the one who sat on the shoulder of Jesus for a time telling him who *he* was. Ask John the Baptist. He knew, perhaps even before Jesus did, that God was *here* in the flesh of this man. From the time he kicked his mother's womb inside out, John had the sense of the immediacy of, as he called it, God's *reign*. It's here! It's here! He screamed, crazy, immoderate, burning, alive. The time has come! It is *now*, not then! The place has come! It is *here*, not there! Make straight the way of the Lord. Ask *him*—that John—if you dare.

Ask me what? What it's like to grow up with a cousin who turns out to be God's son? How nice, you say, to have so close a call from the Lord most high. God is so distant, you complain. Listen, you're lucky. He can come *too* close. You think I like my life? You think it's easy, living as if there were nothing else but God? No family, no wife, no career, no children, no future, no friends. Who could be friends with me? There is no relaxing in the kingdom of God. I know nothing else. I run around, half-crazy, trying to wake people up, trying to turn them around, trying to tell them what I see. What I see is the Lord—*here*, not *there*! Near! Closer than anyone ever thinks. Closer than your very breathing. Closer than your wife. Closer than I am to you. Closer than now is to here. Pay attention! Pay attention!

When I think of John the Baptist I remember myself when I am passionate. There is a pain about him. A poignancy. A desperation. And, finally, a great and pervasive melancholy, which I recognize as my own. He was the first Irish monk. John the Baptist, as the Church remembers him and as I imagine him, reveals the *totality* of demand that God's reign makes upon the person it claims. Something there is in John that makes me want to accuse God of arrogance. But something else there is that makes me understand it is not God's arrogance I fear, but his *presence.* I remember John as a victim of God's close call. When I flee the Lord or myself, when I am angry at what God's call has done to me, at what I have done with rigid piety to myself, blaming him, I remember John. His obsession. His passion. His single-mindedness. I love him, partly for his melancholy, but mainly for his refusal to be on the edge of the crowd. He was no marginal man, that Baptist. He made his name by calling people in from the margin, in from safety, in from detachment. He called them into the center, into conversion, into repentance, into readiness. He made them wet with his own water, his own fury, his own fountain. *The water's fine,* he hollered; *come on in*! The glory of John the Baptist lies in the fact that he was the one who called Jesus in from thirty years on the crowd's edge, in from the margin, in from safety, in from detachment. The glory of John the Baptist—he called Jesus into Christ. If he could do it for him, he can do it for us.

I have a hunch about John; I think he was a real doubter. I think that, sometimes at least, he faked his passion, his zeal, his fire. I think there were days when he left the hairshirt at home, when the whole thing was like revival time down south. I think John the Baptist was like Marjoe or me or any number of splendid preachers who don't believe a word of it! And who discover it doesn't matter that they don't. At some point every preacher must face the horrible and humiliating fact that the people who believe care not at all if you do. Their faith depends and feeds upon God's Word, not yours. The next discovery waiting to be made—Marjoe didn't make it, John did, I am looking still—is that God is so *totally* present to us he is present even in and with and through our disbelief. It was in John's doubting, more than in his zeal, that God drew close to him. In his failure to believe John asked Jesus from prison once more who he was. And Jesus told John in his doubting what he had never told him in his enthusiasm—that he was the suffering servant of Isaiah.

Closer than you think, John said, is this reign, this God, this lamb. Not in that holiness there, but in this sin here. Not in that piety there, but in this doubt. Not in that hope, but in this cynicism. I am dying in jail, angry, bitter and alone; is *this* the reign as well? To say God is here, after all, is to say God is *here*. Where *we* are. Where John was. And, finally, near the end, when John was pushed from the center by Jesus himself to the margin known as prison, Jesus was more obsessed by him than ever, ready to weep and calling him the greatest man who ever kicked a mother's womb.

Speaking for myself, what I would like to learn from John is how to be doubtful and zealous at once. How to be critical *and* committed. How to believe and, so to speak, how to unbelieve. If what John said about the immediacy of God's reign is true, I will meet the Lord *here* wherever that happens to be. Such belief as this allows me to claim my unbelief as an asset — because it is mine. Such faith as this in the *totality* of God's presence allows me to cherish my doubt — because it is mine and is what makes me interesting. Such holiness as this enables me to embrace my sin, without guilt.

What is required to leave the margin, finally, whether of one's life or of an SDS meeting, is the sense that the center will hold even if *you* move to it. With *your* sin and *your* failure and *your* lack of nerve. Our training and our growing and our learned love of inertia conspire to keep us marginal by claiming that the center is reserved for those who have no doubts and those who are not critical. But the sense grows on us that people who are doubtless and uncritical are less wise than dangerous. John reveals to me that I am not only worthy of the center but needed by it.

When I have my periodic attack of self-doubt I am deprived sometimes of the luxury of guilty withdrawal by the memory of John's wild crying. It was when Jesus joined him at the center by the river and John, thinking of his sin, said, "Oh, let me out of here. I can't even tie your shoes." To which Jesus replied only with a bowed head, waiting for water. *If I am worthy to baptize God, what can't I do? If God is crazy enough to come to me, why should I be sane?*

What, really, are the effects of all this on our lives? As far as I can tell, looking at my own life, there are two effects. One is freedom. The other is fear.

Believing in God, finally, is quite the most freeing thing about me. There is something total, something unyielding, something preposterous at the very center of my life. When I dare, having climbed down from my shoulder, to be present to it, everything changes. I am free of my several slaveries; money, success, friendship, sexual intensity, achievement, popularity all lose their terror for me in the shadow of my belief, in the shadow of God's reign over my life. They lose their terror and take on their fitting charm. For example, celibacy, which I love as well as hate, becomes possible even for me—the most moderate, most modern of people. Celibacy becomes possible as freedom and as radicalism itself, even for me. Celibacy is one of the ways I pay attention to the unyielding holy nearness around which I am building a life. And voluntary poverty, the end of ownership, is something like that too. Even for me, the most acquisitive of squirrels.

God's presence to his people is not moderate, not sophisticated, not restrained, not detached. And so John the Baptist was not a moderate man. God's presence to his people is an extreme demand for an extreme response. That is the truth of what I have found. It's what the old saints meant when they said God wants it all, not to obliterate it but to fulfill it. Our trouble —my trouble—is that, for now, obliteration and fulfillment look so much alike.

And so the second effect of this Baptist way of life is fear. Suspicion. The worry that we are

being foolish or neurotic or Calvinist or something. We may be less afraid of the devil than of
our own failed toilet training, but we are afraid.
What if, having embraced the cause, having
moved to the center, I sacrifice my doubt?
What if, having been saved, I lose my right to
sin? What if, having overcome inertia, I make a
mistake, look foolish or, worse, turn out to be a
mediocre success? What if, having believed in
God, as Bernstein's boy-celebrant puts it, God
doesn't believe in me?

Beyond these questions there remains a fear
that refuses to be specified. It may be only the
stunned fear and trembling that holy people report as part of the price of being close to God.
It may be only the infant-fear of not having
one's way. It is the fear of silence and loneliness
and the fear that the God who claims to be both
Word and Love lies. I am most afraid, I know,
of that. I am most afraid of never speaking or
writing again, of losing the gift of words. I am
most afraid of discovering finally that I am
alone. This is the fear that the nearness of God
stirs in me. If you do not feel it, you know too
little of God's silence, too little of his solitude.

We have been talking about conversion. Radical change. Being turned around. Moved
beyond. *Metanoia*. John represents the conver-

58

sion to immediacy: the immediacy of God to
our lives and the immediacy of *ourselves* to our
lives. *Immediacy* is Latin for *face-to-face.* No
go-betweens. No diplomats. No hired represen-
tatives between us. We are both *here,* not there.
God, as Robert Ochs puts it, is more present
than we think. Which is another way of saying
that *we* are too.

The conversion to immediacy is the experience of God's *immoderate* presence. God is not
detached, cool, aloof, shoulder-sitting. God is
not moderate: God is an extreme demand for an
extreme response. John the Baptist would never
have made it at Harvard or any of the places
where "moderation" is held up as an ideal or
personified by such moderates as MacNamara,
Moynihan and Kissinger. Holiness is the op-
posite of inertia, and is more characterized by
bold radicalism, religiously, politically, socially,
than by, say, benign neglect. *That* is what John
says to us with his life and death.

The conversion to immediacy is the conversion of God's absence into a form of presence.
God is so totally present that when he appears
not to be here, he is. God's nearness is not a
matter of the sacred, the silent, the "religious"
or the "moral." God's nearness is a matter, as
John discovered, of desert sand, of grasshop-
pers, of the king's lovely daughter and of a rival

cousin. God's nearness is a matter of day-to-day, face-to-face living. For example, God's nearness is a matter of my own failed sermon; sometimes the Lord comes to us disguised as embarrassment. What we all thought was mere nervousness in my voice—perhaps it was fear and trembling.

What I am calling the conversion to immediacy leads to urgent political action. John's call to repentance and its secular equivalent, the call to humane revolution, is how we attend to the *presence* of God and our best selves in and through the structures of society. Every conversion has its *political* consequences, and the conversion to immediacy means that citizens will not surrender control of their lives to the leprechauns who live on society's shoulders. The people refuse to accept their perennial role as the observers of power at work; the people participate in the exercise of power. I do. You do. It is a matter of discovering that *we* are the fabled "people" in whose name everybody tries to speak. From now on we speak for ourselves.

What I am calling the conversion to immediacy leads also to a deep and quiet prayer — which is speaking for oneself to God. Prayer becomes attention to *presence*—not only God's, but one's own. For, remember, this conversion is a turning not only to God, but to oneself. The transcendent, which we so neglect and for which we have such deep yearning, is not only where God lives, but where *we* live when we are most alive. Our commitment to the transcendent is the refusal to allow the best years of our lives to happen without us. Prayer is how that refusal occurs daily. Prayer is how we respect the transcendent God and the transcendent self which meet for us in the experience of *presence*, of being *here*, not *there*.

At this point the words begin to fail us, quite clearly failing me as a writer and you as a reader. What the hell, after all, does any of this *mean*? At this point, the point of mystery in its refusal to be described, we prepare as always to fall silent. There is failure here; if we were more attentive and better at expressing ourselves, we could push the covers back a bit on truth. We can't. I can't. It is a familiar limit and an old failure. No surprise. It is at this point that lovers turn to flesh and Christians to bread. Here preachers often turn to the old tricks and the pat phrases. Here everyone turns to the wistful daydream. Everyone claims to know the rest, when none of us do. I am trying to let our common act of falling silent be more than failure this time, more than surrender, more than fear. Could it be some awe, the beginnings of worship? Could it be prayer?

What did you go out to the desert to see? A prophet? Yes. And more than a prophet. What did you go out to see? A man? Yes. And more than a man. But what did you go out to see? God? Yes. And more.

5
A Conversion to Humor

We have it in us to laugh only at what is deadly serious. The comic figure of our age has been General Jack D. Ripper whom you will remember as the Strangelove character who "nuked" Russia without proper authorization. That was in the early sixties. The Pentagon, offended, objected to the movie's ridicule and then proceeded to spend a decade making its own version of military burlesque in Southeast Asia, where it went in search of corners to turn and tunnels for there to be light at the end of. By the early seventies our military leaders and their civilian "bosses" still looked like John Wayne and Jimmy Stewart, but they had begun to talk like Chill Wills, Peter Sellers and Woody Allen. In the early sixties we laughed at the thought of total war and felt guilty for laughing, as if it were irreverent. A decade later, having waged a war that has been all too "total" for many Vietnamese and many Americans, a war that resists all our powers of resistance, we suspect that laughter is not irreverent, but the only response available to us, short of going mad.

During the winter of 1972, driving back from a Harrisburg Eight rally on Pennsylvania's horrible Route Seven, my two friends and I were in an automobile accident. It was snowing lightly. Our small car spun out and we began bouncing all over the highway, between guard-rails and tractor-trailer trucks. Though we were going fifty miles an hour, I experienced the careening and banging and turning as if it were happening in slow motion. In my head there was even a musical soundtrack accompanying the crashing, and though I don't remember what the song was, the effect on me was similar to the absurd conclusion of Dr. Strangelove, in which a two-minute sequence of nuclear explosions are set off to the tune of *We'll Meet Again.*

When the car came to rest we were right side up and blocking two lanes of high-speed truck traffic. I looked up to two sets of headlights careening toward us out of the wet night. I knew I had time either to say an act of contrition or to scream, "Goddammit, Dave, move!" I think I screamed: "Goddammit, Dave, I am heartily sorry!" My friend the driver, though bleeding profusely, popped the car into gear. We limped off the roadway just as two Pentagon-sized trucks passed us on their way to heaven. We were no sooner safe than the engine died.

I looked at my friends. One was bleeding from his face, but all right. The other was dazed but conscious. I knew immediately that I was not hurt. And I knew I was going to cry. I jumped out of the car, ostensibly to check for fire, but really to weep alone. But as the sobs made their way up my throat, they experienced a conversion of their own with which I had nothing to do. All my dread and all my terror came rushing out of my body as great uproarious laughter. I turned my face upward to the snow and the night, I stretched out my arms, and I laughed and I laughed and I laughed.

It was a moment in which I seized my entire life by the shoulders and shook it, as I was seized myself by the luck and the absurdity and the pain and the pure pleasure of survival. I was responding ignobly to the accident, but to so much more than the accident. It was a moment in which my whole life was summed up. I was responding to all of my accidents rolled into one. All of my life's collisions flashed before me: my patriotic origins against my Harrisburg fear of the government; my penchant for success against my membership in a failing priesthood; my ease with friends against my loneliness; my love of yesterday against my work for the revolution; my addiction to Jesus against my disdain for the Church; my chosen celibacy against my yearning for a family of my own; my dread seriousness against my impish and foolish humor. I crashed on myself and I laughed and I laughed and I laughed.

There was no one to slap me, to bring me back to my senses, saying, as if I were Humphrey Bogart imitating Woody Allen, "Thanks. I needed that." But in fact what I needed was given me. It was laughter, which poured over me like ointment, healing, allowing me comfort and rebellion at once. Yes, I am embarrassed to remember that my first thought was *not* for my friends. Yes, I am lucky that they were not hurt more seriously. Yes, I confess that in a moment of crisis I was utterly selfish; I confess it as a sin in some way. But not in a way that denies the importance for my salvation—which is to say, service and happiness—of what happened in that moment of collision. My guard was pulled down by a brush with death. I met myself in my own absurd and naked and mixed-up vulnerability, and in the meeting I was converted, changed, moved beyond to something new about life and God. I met myself and I was funny as hell. I laughed and I laughed and I laughed.

What little redemption I experience in my life has come to me in the experience of myself as buffoon. As foolish. As funny. As embarrassing to myself. The pleasure of that experience is matched only by the pleasure of discovering that the community I cherish most—the Church —has itself the secret character of buffoon, of fool, of funny-folk. Nowhere is this more clearly revealed than in the person of the Church, which from its earliest days has chosen as its own central metaphor the figure of Simon Peter, fisherman.

It is commonplace to talk of Jesus as a clown, but he was nowhere near as hilarious, foolish, funny, grave-merry as was Simon Peter. As I discovered on Route Seven that night, laughter is what happens when we survive collisions. No one in the Scriptures survives more collisions than Peter. His was a role that couldn't be played straight. He was the occasion of the first mother-in-law joke. Simon Peter, perfect for Peter Sellers.

In the Roman Catholic tradition of the Church we talk about Peter as if he were the first pope, triple tiara, Mercedes-Benz, infallibility and all. "On this rock . . . never the gates of hell . . . etc." But in every story about Peter there is always a counterpoint, a paradox, a laugh. The only infallible thing about *this* fisherman was his ability, when life was going well, to blow it. And so it was that, as the Church remembers in Matthew, no sooner had Peter been handed the keys of the kingdom than he began to drop them.

Jesus was going on from his lavish praise of Peter to say that the first consequence of that kingdom—its first key—was suffering and death. Jesus was on his way to Jerusalem and the hill of skulls. Peter, it seemed, wanted to go directly to Rome and to institutionalized privilege. And so, "taking Jesus aside, he started to remonstrate with him." Don't go. No, you don't. Uh-huh, Lord. We'll just by-pass the death bit. The suffering. The poverty.

To which Jesus replied to his holiness, "Get behind me, Satan! You are my enemy. The way you think is not God's but man's!" And on the day of his coronation!

Ouch! A moment for Oliver Hardy. The collision of high-flown rhetoric and petty fear. There would be no by-passing: it was not Monopoly. Peter was always there with the wrong word and the slightly miscalculated gesture. But it was a collision he survived. And Matthew has him immediately up the hill of transfiguration with James and John, who knew enough to keep their mouths shut when Jesus was showing off. But not Peter. "Hey, that's terrific, Lord! How about pitching our tents right here, huh?" Slap. No. Let's go.

Peter trails along behind Jesus all the way to Jerusalem, always trying to win him over, always failing, foolishly. Walking on the water like a Looney-Tune figure, until he noticed what he was doing and—whooooooooop—nearly drowned. He could go from magnificence to pettiness in an instant. And survive.

It was the night before Jesus died and, like any man, he found it hard to tell his friends he loved them. And so he got water, some soap and a towel. He started to wash their feet, taking their dirt and ugliness and bad smell as a final memory. Until he got to Peter. Peter alone was too humble to be washed by the Lord; "Not *my* feet, you don't, Lord. Uh-huh!"

"If not, Peter, you and I are through."

"Well, hell, Jesus, then not just my feet but my armpits as well, and behind my ears and between my teeth!" All or nothing, that was Peter, who wanted it both ways and usually got it neither. He could go from arrogance to embarrassment in an instant. And survive. It is why we love him so.

The ultimate humor of Simon Peter comes

on the night of his deepest tragedy. It is the co-incidence of the funny and the brutal that makes us silent. (Remember Howard Cosell in Woody Allen's *Bananas* doing the play-by-play of an assassination? Remember the same Cosell a few months later reporting live the deaths of Israeli athletes at Munich? And Haywood Hale Broun, for God's sake.) There are moments when the world demands tears *or* laughter from us and cares not which, since they become the same thing when deeply felt. And so it was that when everyone else was saying, "Is it I, Lord?", Peter, picking his teeth, said, "Even if I have to die with you I shall never disown you!" It was the very night of his betrayal, not once, not twice, but—count 'em—three times. And the cock laughed. And Peter got out of the wreckage, stunned again at his survival, and turned his face up to the night and he cried and he cried and he cried. It is not an unfamiliar moment.

Peter can be a figure of laughter for us, finally, because Jesus survived the collision of life and death. We remember his survival as the resurrection, which the Church Fathers called the "laughter of God." The final comic story of the Gospel is the densely human moment of reconciliation between Peter and Jesus which is tacked onto John's narrative as an appendix.

An epilogue. A last word. A final joke.

In the dim light of dawn Jesus appears on the shore, and from their boat someone screams, "It is the Lord!" And then, in a subtle and gratuitous Chaplinesque, John gives us the gift of this magnificent detail: "At these words 'It is the Lord,' Simon Peter, who had practically nothing on, wrapped his cloak round him and jumped into the water." An instant replay of the first failed water-walk. Try, try again. And with his coat *on*! Like the Labor Day clowns at the neighborhood swimming pool, off the high-dive, fully clothed. Deadly serious. Earnest. The classic fool.

When Jesus, in the anticlimax of their first greeting, asks for a fish or two for breakfast, Peter drags ashore "one hundred and fifty-three of them." Picture him, soaking wet, panting, aching, standing silent before Jesus, desperate for approval, forgiveness, acceptance. A returned puppy. Not one fish, not two. But— count 'em—one hundred and fifty-three!

And finally, after the pained silence of the meal in which no one dared ask Jesus how he was or even who he was, Jesus spoke to Peter. It was like a shot: "Simon, son of John, do you love me?" Oh, Lord, God, damn, here it is, the moment, the question, everything turning. "Yes, Lord, you know I love you." Then, three times: I love you. I love you, you know.

Peter subdued at last? Tamed? Housebroken? No longer the fool? Not quite. The last moment of the good news story, as Jesus walks off into the sunset with Peter, is a moment of pettiness and jealousy and warm humor at the end. It was John who beat Peter in the race to the tomb on Sunday. And now John, who claims the title "Beloved of Jesus," horns in on the glorious intimacy of Peter's reconciliation with his Lord. As John follows them Peter says, "What's with him, Lord?" To which Jesus replies in his last words according to the Gospel of John, "What's it to you?" Ouch! Oh my! Did it again.

And Peter went on doing it again, losing arguments with Paul and getting lost on the way to Rome and, finally, even at the end, managing his fate with pride enough to die on a cross like Jesus did, and foolishness enough to do it upside down.

We have been talking about conversion, about *metanoia,* being changed, moved beyond, turned around. Laughter is one of the ways in which that happens. Every laugh is a small conversion, a moment of turning, a moment when we summon up from well below our surfaces an affirmation. We are *always* going from the glorious to the mundane, from the marvelous to the mediocre. And our laughter says it is all right for us to do so. It is all right for us to fail, to falter. When the collisions of our existence get the best of us, we stop being funny; we begin to act as if nothing new can happen, as if we *cannot* fall or blow it or trip. As if *this* is all that is possible. *That* is giving up, sitting down, stopping. Inversion, not conversion.

The redemption of our current predicaments is that they are so totally unpredictable. The ridiculous and the absurd and merely silly—they are all always leaping out of God-knows-where at us, demanding that we look again before giving up. There is more than death here, it says; there is survival. There is more than importance here; there is whimsy. There is always the unnecessary. Laughter is the signal of grace—the ultimate unpredictability.

This is not meant to be an essay on humor, but only my testimony that humor is what saves me from myself, from my melancholy, from my disappointment and from my rage. I trip a lot, for example. Not completely by accident, as my astute friends know. It is not just that I am phony or falsely clownish, but that I need continually to remind myself and my companions that none of this matters, after all, you know. Not really, not finally. Not, I mean, ultimately.

Not even what angers me or depresses me most. None of what I do or worry about is beyond laughter. Only my dead seriousness is deadly. And so, ooops, I trip a lot. I pretend in my sophistication to be a fool. And now and then, when I need it most, my real foolishness leaps out at me and I am ready to laugh or cry, like a child whose balloon has just escaped to heaven. Laugh or cry. Dance or mourn. If we are capable of one we are capable of the other. It is the paralysis that refuses both that we must resist with all our might. And with all our studied tripping.

What shall I compare this generation to? It is like the children who would not dance when I piped. It is like the people who would not laugh when I tripped. Who would not cry when I played the dirge-music.

Speaking for myself, I would like to be compared to Peter, who *always* responded. It is true that on most days he got it wrong. But he tried, and we remember him at least for his mistakes. When Jesus piped a joyful tune for him, Peter went into mourning. And when Jesus played a dirge, Peter always danced. He got it wrong, upside down, coat on instead of off. And that is why I cherish him.

In secret I get it wrong too. I need to believe that Jesus, or the world at least, can live with me like this. I need to believe that Jesus, or the world at least, will survive *me, my* foolishness, *my* incompetence, *my* cowardice. I think of myself on a tightrope with a jar full of nitroglycerine; if I fall everything will blow up. And so, of course, I *do* fall, and everything survives because it was not nitroglycerine at all but Jello, J-E-L-L-O. The world has survived the explosion, but will I survive the humiliation of taking a jar of Jello so seriously?

I always have so far. I have survived all my grandiosity, all my falls, and all my jars of Jello. Indeed—and this is what matters—I have not only survived. I have laughed my ass off. Sometimes crying.

Perhaps God tries to tell us something. I mean with all our falls and all our nitro-jello and all the deadly seriousness of death that turns out to be life and all the ways we get funnier by the day. At the deepest level to which I can descend I discover my own response to my own piping to be laughter. It is an affection I have for myself. It is a way I have of forgiving myself. It is a way I have of enjoying myself. It is a way I have of being enjoyed. And, more important, being forgiven. Not everything of this laughter is lovely or light. There are times when it nearly kills me. At times I am humiliated by it.

When I went to jail for the Vietnamese, I was all courage, principle, outrage and crucifixion. The night in jail was awful. My cell was wet from an overflowing toilet and from the cowardice I could not flush away. By the time I got to the judge I said, hating myself, that I was sorry for putting everybody out, and someone in the courtroom laughed at me. So sometimes there is this self-contempt, and laughter has its way then as well. Being funny is not all that funny. As Peter could tell you, I'm sure. He had his day in court too. There are times when I choose not to be compared to that cowardly incompetent. Usually when I am hiding from someone I love and whom, for that reason, I have betrayed.

Still, if I took Genesis at its word and claimed to be an image of God, it would be in my laughing that I would do so. For everything I would like God to say of himself is true of me then—dare I claim it? Though laughter is my sin at times, it is also my closest call to the love of uselessness, the unconditional acceptance, the pure forgiveness, the freedom, the creativity, the integrity that God is if he is what we crack him up to be. Perhaps God tries to tell us in our laughter what he is like. Maybe that is why I would rather laugh at myself in the company of friends than anything in the whole world.

I asked for forgiveness of my companions in jail by telling them later of my grand foolishness and asking them to laugh at me and to let me laugh with them. They love me and so, though no one said it was that important, it happened. Maybe laughing so in the company of friends is what God longed for when he made the world in the first place. If so I understand him better all the time. I hope it's true; I could love a God who was so much like myself.

Then again, I *have* been wrong. It *is* possible that God is more like a Latin American dictator than he is like me. If so, I could live with that too. In fact, if my premise is true that humor is the product of collisions, and laughter is how we survive them, then God will be as much like me as nitroglycerine is like Jello. I am in no hurry to find out.

In the meantime, I survive. I leave the wreckage. I go aside to be alone. I put my coat on and jump in. I walk the water and sink. I surprise myself continually by being right when I am ready to be wrong. And when I am most desperate and hungry and lonely for myself, if not for God, I go to the nearby tower, thinking of death. I climb and, tripping, only half on purpose, I fall from the third step and lay there and I laugh and I laugh and I laugh. It is what little I know yet, since I am not yet there, of Easter.

6
The Converted Church

When I see him I pull off the road, stop, wave, open the door and shout, "Hi! Come on! Get in!"

"Thanks, Mister," he says, hair blowing. He throws his faded orange knapsack in the back.

"Where you headed?" I ask.

"Damascus," he replies.

"What?" I say.

"Not only that," he says. "God knocked me off my horse. I'm blind. I was persecuting him and he came to me."

"He did?" I say, thinking, is he a mugger or what?

"My name," he says, "is Saul."

To which I reply, hitting sixty, "Far out."

The figure of Saul-turned-Paul rides with me sometimes. Some days I yearn to be like him,

79

to have his thick experience behind me. To be the Norman Mailer of the New Testament. To have known the crystal moment of such conversion as his. What purity! What clearheadedness! From his horse yet! And the voice of God! I would go blind for a while gladly if it meant that eventually I would see without this fog.

All this time I have been talking about conversion, *metanoia,* turning around, moving beyond, radical change. But what do I know? I have never been knocked from *my* horse. I have been changed, but not like that. You have probably been waiting for me to clear things up, to say right out what I mean. But I'm simply not up to it. To be honest, I don't ride a horse, though I fancy myself a cowboy now and then. You see, the conversions I claim have left me confused, not clear. Indeed my conversions have *cost* me clarity. Maybe I *am* blind and this is the time of re-focus.

Conversion—having worked very hard all my life to be a "success," a "good priest," a "published poet," a "favored son," "smart," I woke up one morning and found that none of it meant a damn thing. It was like falling out of bed.

Conversion—having spent all my energy trying to win my friends to my side and keep them in a circle around me, I kept waking up alone. It was like losing an election, though everybody said they voted for you.

Conversion—having knelt down twice a day all those years, God rewarded my piety and came to me at last. But he took me up a hill and asked me, if I had a child, would I kill it for him? I said no. I haven't seen God since. It was like falling out of Eden.

Conversion—having been chaplain to a clinic for alcoholics and then to a great university, I forgot one day which was which, and then, one day, whether I was the professor, the patient or the priest. It was like losing your place in a book you were writing.

You are probably wondering by now whether I have had a conversion or a breakdown. If so, we are understanding each other. I keep picking up the hitchhiker Saul because he knew how to talk about his breakdown as if it were a conversion. He talked about his fall as if it were a flight. That's what I am trying to do.

The conversions we seek are, at their root, preparations for the one great change of heart in which we give ourselves to God. The changes we detect in our lives up to now will be as nothing compared to that change. Our problem is not that we are incapable of the great and final conversion, but that our small and mediocre conversions in the meantime will seem unimportant to us. After all, we do not fall from horses.

The Lord never speaks to us. We are not blinded.

Then again, from another angle, the story of Paul, even in its details, has happened to us. I'm thinking of the conversion we have experienced together as Church. Paul is a figure, if not of me, of me and you together. He is a figure of the converted Church.

At the beginning of the story, like ourselves in all our beginnings, Saul was smug and certain in the knowledge of his ways. On St. Stephen's day Saul held the murderer's coats. He knew what he was doing. He was getting ready to defend the truth with his life and proclaim it by taking the lives of other people. Such certainty! Saul did not know the difference between faithfulness and arrogance. Saul reveals that belief without an edge of doubt is not only transitory but dangerous.

Then one day, dramatically and violently, his faith fell apart. Saul became Paul by being confronted with his own misguided zeal, by seeing the false wisdom that loves to kill for truth, by opening his eyes to his own sin. What he saw broke his eyes and his heart. He was not the man he thought he was. He was not so tough. He was the terrible beast that in its heart was helpless, looking for help from the people he pursued. It was a traumatic moment: not just the shaking of his identity with right-wing Israel, not just the collapse of his law and order impulses, but the revelation of his own deep, dark, perverse weaknesses.

There is an irony here. We are always talking about conversion as if it happened to holy folks. Conversion happens only to the grotesque. Only to the coat-holders of this world.

The Church is always a prime candidate for conversion. Though, in our common talk about ourselves, we seem to be good and holy enough, we are and have been the coat-holders to murder's modern forms. Need we count the ways? I didn't think so. The Church, ourselves together, is in its heart something helpless looking for help. And what is peculiar to our time is the way we are living in touch with that embarrassment. The conversions have done this to us. We have lost our claim to smugness because now we know so little and our ignorance is so public. We have lost our claim to arrogance because we are so visibly unfaithful, even to our minor promises. We have lost our claim to innocence by being exposed as active participants in the contemporary assault—to mention only one—on women's rights and other works of Mary. Oh, ourselves the Church! What are we if not down from our high horse and blind? What are we saying to God and each other if not, "What wilt thou have me to do?"

The major problem with conversions like this one is the lack of home it leads to. When Saul became Paul he was forever in search then for what he had as a young man—a clear fellowship of righteousness. He never found it, for all his travels, for all his badgering Corinth. I have been trying to tell you what *metanoia* has been like in my life. Its troublesome effect has been this awful homelessness. I have touched my own hidden helplessness and, in being terrible, I am only looking for help. I look, say, to the Church for help, but it is helpless too and that is why the Church is terrible to me.

All my lovely talk about being changed and deepened comes down on Tuesday, say, to the fact that I am continually in trouble. Not for doing anything outrageous, particularly. But for saying what I think. I am, off and on, in trouble with my community, with the bishop, with my family, with some old friends. Mainly I am in trouble with myself. I don't like being on the ground, blind, waiting for the horse to kick me in the head. I don't know where else to go and for now there is no one to help me up and point me on the way. Not even a seeing-eye dog. It is a very lonely feeling.

I am probably overdoing it. My self-sorry feelings are always trying to tip my hand on me.

All I am trying to say is that being changed like we have been means the loss of some comfort, means we no longer fit neatly into previous niches, institutions or ways of acting. We have been calling our deep experience of change *conversion,* but some people, bureaucrats and authoritarian administrators, for example, call it *breakdown.* Either word will do. What we know for sure is that our soul is not the same. We are not the people we thought we were. We are professors, patients and priests at once. But we insist on our right to be here, however we are. The bureaucrats and overseers wish we'd go away. In fact on some days they tell us to get out. Now if it was the army or, say, the Environmental Protection Agency, they would be right. Conversions and/or breakdowns not allowed. But this is Church. I come here to pray, Fadda, not to fight. Not to stamp papers. I come here because I've got a big question for God, which is: "What wilt thou have me to do?" Church is where and with whom we ask that question. And Church would be better off if it understood that *it* must ask the question also. Repeatedly.

One of the great and painful ironies of our day is that many of us, in the experience of shattering if not dramatic conversion, find ourselves in danger of being alienated from the community, language and tradition we need most. We find ourselves wondering if our conversion to Jesus Christ is costing us the Church. For some of us that is precisely the case; in the pursuit of real prayer and real involvement in the resistance of evil in its current forms, our very own cherished tradition has fought us, embarrassed us, sought to turn us out. But we are not gone. We have not left the Church and we will not. God may be an ex-Catholic, but I am not. I have a right to be here.

Why am I surprised at the difficulty of our days? Because, like every child, I want it both ways. I want to be changed, but I want you to be the same. I want to be turned around without pain. I want to be allowed my sin, but I want you to be pure. I want conversion without conflict. I want to be tough but I want only gentleness from you. The Church, in its bureaucrats, administrators and saints, is right to force the desert on us. Paul knew; he got up from the ground, blind, and spent the next period of his life a wandering Jew, desert-bound. It is a feeling we have come to know. We just don't like it yet.

Paul is a figure of the conversion we seek, not just because we can identify with his trauma and his suffering, but mostly because the effect in him of the trauma and the suffering was so splendid. He was not obsessed, as we so often are—as I am—by what transformation costs in pain, loneliness and lost certainty. Paul was clear why death made a home in his body—so that the life of Jesus could be seen. He was clear why his credentials as a religious leader and a good Jew were taken from him—so that God could be his one credential and the love of his friends his only letter of recommendation. Paul was clear why he was mocked as a fool and buffoon by authorities—so that the wisdom of God could be revealed.

My own wish to be like Paul really amounts to my wish that I could learn to love my weaknesses as a source of strength.

I think of the time I went to work as a chaplain at a clinic for alcoholics. Oh, I arrived pure, powerful, sober as hell. I had learned my lessons well; I was healer, reconciler, articulator of hope for the despairing. Good news . . . chaplain is a'comin'. I wore the clerical version of a white hat—a black suit. I was going to be the one priest who didn't pass by on the way to the temple, but who reached down, Samaritan-like, to pull the poor bugger out of his gutter.

But the poor buggers wouldn't come. If I was ever knocked from a horse, it was when I discovered the patients of that clinic didn't think I was terrific. They got a bead on me and opened fire. I was ridiculed, laughed at, ignored, attacked, mocked and patronized by wily alcoholic men and women whose other addiction was to the truth. Who the hell are you to offer cures? Who are you to come here nine to five with your studied compassion? An old drunk named Bobby looked right through me one day, saying, "Jim boy, you need a drink." And he was right. And that night I went to a bar and got drunk for the first time in my life. At dawn I was walking along a Georgia railroad track, looking for a boxcar to sleep in.

I never told them about that, but those wily alcoholic men and women knew. They knew before I did what it was the eyes I had by then were seeing. All at once we stopped being patients, priests and poor buggers to each other. I lost a whole set of credentials only to discover that there are other credentials, written not with ink but with the Spirit of the living God, not on stone tablets, but on the fleshy tablets of living hearts. The great and stunning lesson I learned from Bobby and his companions is that my fellowship in loneliness and my nearness to the chaos that leads to, among other things, addiction, is precisely the gift they needed from me most. My presence at the clinic was useful and healing and important because I was forced into the reluctant fellowship of uselessness, sickness and insignificance. It was a matter of getting knocked off one's (high) horse. A Georgia hillbilly played the Lord to my Saul. I learned something about the happy fault, about vessels of clay, about thorns in the flesh that will not be forgotten.

Conversion? It is the fellowship of dust we share when we say with each other: "We are in difficulties on all sides, but never cornered; we see no answer to our problems, but never despair; we have been persecuted but never deserted; knocked down, but never killed. It is all God's work. It was God who reconciled us to himself through Christ and gave us the privileged work of handing on this reconciliation."

If the reconciliation looks like defeat? What then? If the conversion looks like breakdown? If the fellowship feels like loneliness? We must be wary of glib and holy words in which the fearful are always hiding from their fears. I am not appealing to the "Scriptures" or to "the apostle of the Gentiles," but to Paul, a man whom I met in Bobby the drunk, whom I meet in myself. His language, his urging, his hope come of the same frightened desperation we know. If he were alive with us now, he would not be pope or patriarch or oracle of wisdom. He would be one of us; he would be now as he was then, slightly in trouble with the authorities, irrascible to the monkish ones, irreverent to the liturgists, and imprudent to the canonists.

If we are trying to come to grips now with the alienating aspects of the changes we detect in ourselves—alienating from our traditions, families, bosses, career, goals and part of ourselves —Paul is a crucial figure for us. He was able to live with profound alienation from his own past while resisting the self-serving temptation to the "cult of alienation," which was an option even then. Paul was never alienated from the community of believing *people*, nor from the Lord in whom he believed with closed eyes. He took no pleasure in his suffering, as we are wont to do. He did not seek martyrdom, nor even jail. He was courageous enough to be openly a coward, and he was self-accepting enough to accept the weaknesses, hypocrisies and failures in faith of his fellows. The great temptation of Paul's life must have been to get back on that horse (high) and lord it over everyone again. He says to me, as I seek martyrdom or alienation for its own sake or smug certainty in my rebellion, "Watch it; you're climbing that horse (high) again." He says it with a kind of clarity one only expects from drunkards. I *do* need a drink, you see. I hope I never forget.

The Church allows me to remember. It is

mysterious to everyone but me why I am still in the Church. I am here because my drinking isn't bad enough yet to require the clinic. I am here because my horse got away. I am here because the Church in its brokenness faces me with my own. More than that, the Church demands of me that I not worship my brokenness but see in it how I am whole. The Church admits sin but moves beyond it by instinct to the promise of reconciliation. It *fits* me to be part of this people—much in the way that the city with its wretched streets fits me better than the pastures of Vermont.

I am off my horse. I am on the road. I am in the streets. There are ghettos here. There is dust. There are muggers in the shadows. There are victims in the ditches. There is hypocrisy and violence. There is blindness. Beggars are lame. No one has credentials.

There is someone else here, standing up, arms out as if either in prayer or flagging down a ride. It is you. It is Paul. It is all of us. We are going someplace together. Pilgrims. We carry folded tents. We carry whiskey. We ask questions, but never wait for answers. It is an act of hope, hitchhiking. An act of trust. It is dangerous. It is foolish. Sometimes it is against the law. We would not do it, except we are not ready yet to rest. We are not home. We are waiting still for the ride to come, the open door and the voice we long to hear, saying, "Hi. Come on. Get in."

7
A Conversion to Life

Holy Week. The days we dread. A time to go hungry. Palm Sunday, dull Monday, lost Tuesday, Spy Wednesday, Holy Thursday, Good Friday and that Saturday forever. It is the week we would sleep through if we could. But we are too awake. Too ready. Too much alive to ignore such death as these days parade before us. If we dread it, we yearn for it too.

It is the time when the whole world—even we ourselves—stops hiding for once from death. And therefore life is possible. It is the time when Jesus comes out of the back of our year's closet and reminds us that something happened in him that matters still. These are the days when we call his name without fear of being answered except by the silence we seek.

It is important to begin by admitting that I can't stand thinking or talking about death. I don't know how to do it. And so the death of Jesus becomes a product I sell and Holy Week becomes its package and resurrection is the cash being registered.

It is also important to begin by admitting that I never stop thinking and talking about death. It is my one subject; almost all of my stories begin with death or end with it. I have a thing about my own death and I see it happen often, on highways, off bridges, getting shot. And so the death of Jesus is flesh on my bones and Holy Week is when I stand up and resurrection is breath through my lungs. It is why I am still alive. Alle—as they say on Easter—luia. All my talk about changed hearts, conversion, *metanoia* is talk, finally, about Jesus. Death's conversion to life—that is what I mean when I say his name. The ultimate *metanoia*. Holy Week is when all creation has a change of heart. We also call it spring.

I am a grown man, but not now. Not in trying to look squarely in death's face. I am twelve years old, and I am holding my dog Chris in my arms and weeping into his blood and planning to get that mailman who killed my best friend with his darn truck.

I am fourteen, watching my Mom get on a plane, her weeping this time, to go bury Grandma Morrissey.

I am twenty, standing on the curb of Pennsylvania Avenue with two million people, all of us
bawling like babies as Blackjack, the horse
without a rider, struts to the muffled rhythm of
funeral drums and the flagged coffin of Jack
Kennedy passes us.

Since then there has been too much death in
our lives, and not enough. Too many televisions
and not enough faces. We have learned more of
grieving from Walter Cronkite than from our
best loved ones. We were so repulsed by the
manufacture of death in Vietnam when we saw
it in our living rooms that we insisted at first
they put an end to the killing. When the death-
dealing continued we compromised and insisted
only that television stop telling us about it. We
learned in Vietnam how to kill people without
seeing them. We have learned how to keep
death at its distance. It was a valuable lesson,
and now we can even take pleasure in death,
watching its promotion movies and buying its
toys and celebrating the new cult of suicide as if
it were a parlor game. We buy and sell cars now
with Mafia jokes about offers that can't be refused. There is so much death in our lives that
we don't dare deal with it up close, intimately,
touching it. I am a grown man; but growing up
in this age has done this to me: though still I
could weep, I could never hold that bloody dog

Chris in my arms today.

Mary held Jesus in her arms. It is an image we must contemplate, although the mad ones among us smash even Michelangelo's Pieta. We need to know there is another way of living than ours. Another way of dying. What we need to discover is that when death is no longer at a distance, it is life. When we are as close to death as flesh is to flesh, something happens to it that amounts to a change of heart. It is a change in our heart or in the heart of the dead. Death is not the enemy of intimacy; distance is. How do we learn *that* lesson?

By living with Jesus, perhaps, in his dying. Spend a few days in Holy Week this year. For Jesus it was not the liturgical frenzy or the spring vacation or the usual weekday rut that it is for us. For Jesus it was saying farewell to friends. And to an idea of himself. It was one last effort at keeping death at a distance, hoping the cup would spill without his blood. It was facing the fact that this time Time itself had come for him. To collect. To bargain with. To take away. To commit. To finish. To arrest. To kill. Simon Peter was there, speaking as usual for Jesus' own fearful side. And as usual Jesus didn't have the courage it took to be the coward Peter was.

Truth? What is truth? Jesus refused to be

drawn into a discussion with Pilate of epis-
temology and its problems. But would he have
refused to talk about his own death, given the
chance? I remember visiting an old man who
was dying. When I greeted him with a comment
about the weather, he replied, "Hell, preacher.
Don't talk to me about the sunshine. I want to
talk about dyin'. Everybody keeps tellin' me
'bout the sunshine. You tell me about dyin',
hear?"

"Lord, remember me when we're dead." You
and me, fella', Jesus said. We're in this together. Hear?

Death refuses such togetherness. Death is the
bodily experience of betrayal. Jesus' nostrils
were full of that stench in Holy Week: the betrayal of Judas, of course, the near betrayal of
Peter, abandonment by the chosen friends. But
these were as nothing compared to the betrayal
of all one's living that death always seems to be.
Jesus was to die. He flinched at that! He shud-
dered! He turned from it! He said what you will
say on that dread day: "Not me! No!"

"Yes, you. Come on."

"Is that you, God? Not such treason from
you, too?"

"Yes, you. Come on."

"Not me! No! I resist!"

"You are dead. You have no choice."

"Why have you done this to me? Why have you betrayed me, God?"

And then only that vast silence. That eternal silence in which we meet Jesus and glimpse deaths we'd rather keep at a distance.

The silence was broken not by God, but by Jesus. God does not break silences. He breaks only the bodies of his chosen ones, who are always saying, "All right. You win. What's left of me I give to you before you take it. You win." What else is there to say when not only Judas is a Judas, but God is. You have no choice but to trust him. Jesus, when death was no longer *distant* from him, underwent, it seems, a change of heart. When death was close enough for him to be furious and cowardly and "a worm and no man, the reproach of people," then and there he discovered a trust and a faith whose words were, "Into your hands I place what's left of me. I am finished." In the very heart of death he discovered life. Truly this was something, you might have said, of God.

Maybe. Maybe not. If it was of God we will know eventually. If not, that we forgot will not be noticed. At the moment of dying our usual blindnesses are reversed, converted, turned around. Suddenly it is death that is near and life that is distant. In the case of Jesus, distant by

three days or by one's ability to believe the
promise of his last-breath instinct. The promise
that there is something trustworthy in the heart
of death, something you can fight with and lose
to and still love. Resurrection, life, victory,
springtime, open flowers, all of it was there in
the last bloody moment of the man *already*.
Though it would be days growing into words,
the promise of life was in the act of death.
When all the other promises failed, death bore
one more from its own silence. Friday and Sunday: we remember them as if they were years
apart, as if they were the death day, birth day of
two different men. It was all one moment for
Jesus. Ask anyone who was born on the day
they died.

It happened to me in Cleveland. What little I
know of death and resurrection I learned from
Eastern Airlines. It was the moment we dread
in the knowledge that it will come eventually,
whether we are seasoned travelers or not. The
moment when the captain's voice says, cool, detached, distant as death, ". . . emergency . . .
mechanical difficulty . . . prepare . . . oxygen . . .
turning back . . . be calm." I was terrified. We
had twenty minutes in which to gather our be-
longings, to watch the stewardess run through
the drill again, in which to fold the pillow on our

laps, in which to wait for—as they called it—
impact. Twenty minutes in which to remember
how to pray. Twenty minutes to live. Twenty
minutes to die.

Then twelve. I sat alone, looking out the window at the harmless clouds. Funny to come
down from heaven for one's judgment. Go to
earth! I was coming. Twelve minutes and still
without the magic words with which that divine
tenderness would flow over me. I couldn't pray,
beyond my old habits. Hail Mary . . . Oh my
God . . . heartily . . . hardly . . . at the
hour of our death . . . and besides, I want to
live. I want to keep going. I want my life . . .

I found myself talking not to God at all, but
to death: *Look, spare me your sting. Get your
victory off someone else today. Please. Please.* I
found myself talking to my own life: *You were
good to me. What we had was fine. I was hoping it would be more. Hold on to me, please.*

I did not weep. I did not get hysterical. I did
not scream. But I died. No matter that the
landing gear held, that all their safety tricks
worked, that the foam on the runway postponed
the fire until another day. What matters to me
about Cleveland and those twenty minutes,
twelve, seven, three, wheels down, *impact,* is
that I died, no matter what the papers said. By
the time that plane came to a stop at the termi-

nal, I was gone.

And then, on my own third day, I was back. "Grace" is coming out alive when you were down for death. I was reborn because I survived when the landing gear held without my help. There was more than me in that; I was gone and I came back. Resurrection took flesh. My flesh. Resurrection is what happens when we survive what we had no right to. If there is a promise in Cleveland, it is that I who died live. If there is a promise in Holy Week, it is that he who lives died. The moments become the same and we fall silent. Holy Week happens to you all year, and if you are Irish enough, you know it. Easter is what happens when you stand looking back over your shoulder and saying with your silence, "Did I survive *that*? Dear God!"

Look at what you have survived! These years of chaos. The loss of your best friends. The passing of those great moments youth promised you. You have survived your unquenched thirst for truth. You have survived the hardening of your own tenderness. You have survived crash landings, collisions, the deaths of your parents, of your children, of your enemies. You have survived the death of, if not God, your casual friendship with him. You have survived survival. You are alive! And why? For what? By whose order? It is all there in the silence and the laughter which shakes you everytime you do it again—beating death at its own game.

We are always asking God to take the cup away from us. He never does. And so we drink. And we find that it is not blood as we feared, but fine wine. When we anticipate our dread events we are always sure they will kill us. When the dread event arrives, it never does; did I survive *that*? It is the feeling we live for—survival. It is our closest thing to the knowledge of God. The preposterous claim we make in Holy Week is that survival is the central human event; human beings survive everything, including and especially the last death which seems so irrevocable.

These are days when we know what it is to survive. That is the advantage to our chaos and to the danger of our age; we *know* how fragile we are, how fragile is the thin balance that keeps us going. We *know*, as Bernstein's boy-celebrant says, "how easily things get broken." We all live with the gut fear—or is it knowledge?—that the balance has been lost. That globally we are at the threshold of disaster. Some days the only question is what form the world catastrophe will take. And personally, privately, we know what it is to live with an inner momentum toward dissolution, toward despair. We live in touch with the possibilities of our *own* destruction. Some days the only question is whether *we* will go before the world does. And on some days neither question matters. Those are the worst ones.

Who of us can deny knowledge of Holy Week? Of torture? Of betrayal? Of failed farewells? Of utter abandonment? Who claims exemption? We all do, most often. We dare not live in touch with our fragile prospects. We are too close to nothing. We keep not only death at a distance, but our own most hidden selves. But sometimes death insists on its right to be intimate. We cannot hold it off when the plane lurches and hits and screams and the stewardess stops smiling. We cannot hold it off at three o'clock in the morning when your good friend puts down his drink and says, though he seems healthy, "Jim, in my soul, I'm dying." It is the moment when we *know* what it is to *need*. To need a *redeemer,* a savior, a helper, a second, a friend who has extra life to give you. *We need to be redeemed*—it is *the* feeling of our insane and violent age.

We are looking, in our betrayal, for someone to trust. We are looking, in our abandonment, for someone to hold on to. It is now that anger fades and our sophisticated skepticism disappears and we find ourselves surrounded by the old words and rituals. We are looking for hands into which we can commend our spirits. Holy Week is the memory we have that there are hands like that. Jesus is one of us who tells us with his last days what we want to hear.

"Give yourself to God. Never mind who he is. God is life. Give yourself to God and you will live."

The conversion of our death into our life—it is the only conversion, finally, that matters. The ultimate *metanoia*. We are not prepared for it yet because the change of heart required and the loss of heart we risk are too much. We are on the way to life. When you tell me with your friendship that I am *alive* now, I reply that it is as hard for me to believe that I am alive as it is that Jesus rose from the dead. After my long and, in its way, lovely Holy Week, I am an empty tomb to myself. I am a vision of angels, elusive, mysterious, paradoxical, strange. And you are an empty tomb as well. We are this mystery to each other.

But we have still the instincts of Magdalene and Peter. The empty tomb is never a proof to us, but always a promise. It is a promise about Jesus. It is a promise about ourselves. It is where death, having been converted to life, is buried like a seed. The tomb looks empty, dead as any seed. But to eyes like ours it never is. It is full of life.

When we have looked into our hidden and buried selves, expecting to see corpses and failures and defeats, but seeing instead faces of friendly strangers who have made themselves at home, we have a right to go running, glad, with the news. I am neither dead nor alone. When we have looked at these new hearts we bear and found them not lost as we feared, but strong, we should tell each other about it. Our hearts have been changed from stone to flesh.

It is not over. It must happen again. It is the third day only. We will not rest until the seventh. God knows what surprises wait for us. What new ways of coming through death alive. For now the meager ways of our own stories are glorious enough. The past and this wild present are all the training we need for the future's coming. Life is all the preparation we need for death.

We find ourselves in this strange garden, with fallen seeds and silent, sprouting and broken earth. There is agony and blood. There is arrest and sword. The earth breaks with the violence of flowers coming out of their tombs. The earth breaks with burial. You and I may be strangers to each other, but we tend the same green and fragile life. It is the life of Jesus. It is the life we seek. We are gathered in this place of suffering and resurrection. We may be strangers to each other, but in this garden the strangers all resemble God.

At Home in Exile:
Politics, Poetry, Prayer

8
Faithful Politics

We knew in our hearts that Barry Goldwater was almost right. We knew there was some small truth in what he tried in feeble ways to tell us. We have learned since those innocent days what it is: moderation in defense of evil is no virtue. We are, together with Vietnamese men and women, the victims of "moderate" men. Indeed, in our dullness, we are victims of our own "moderation."

Moderation is a word which wears the mask of Aristotle's balanced humanism but which in our peculiar usage refers not to balance but to paralysis. Our problem as a people has boiled down to that—immobility, inaction, impotence. We watched Kitty Genovese in her death struggle. We wrung our hands for a decade over the war that would not end. And now we look on as our cherished ways of worship, of walking, of loving each other all slip away, quiet as nuns leaving convents.

"Among the things Billy Pilgrim could not change," Vonnegut wrote, "were the past, the present and the future." Among the things we cannot change are the systems of corporate power which feed on the hunger of the poor; the preoccupation of religious people with wealth and power; the dividing impulse which separates men into guards and prisoners; the terror of life which makes "protection" the clear priority both in the Pentagon and in night's bedrooms; the loneliness that has us all in the pointless parade through "life-styles," "communes," "open marriages," "liberated zones," "no growth" and "zero population." As if that were our goal.

"Moderation" is our own slick terrorism. Moderate men in business councils, chanceries, newsrooms, studios, bureaucracies, station houses, sacristies, classrooms, taxicabs and air-port bathrooms all conspire in enlightened lan-guage to keep things the same. Everyone tries to get through his term of office without losing the war or winning it. "Moderation" has come to mean irresponsibility; no response. No re-sponse at all. In 1969, telling the truth for once, President Nixon said that he would "under no circumstances . . . be affected whatever" by

protests against the war. Moderation, Viet-
namization, defoliation, decimation, murder.
Words fail us. But only after we fail ourselves.

Another conspiracy stirs up the air, however.
The mingling of age, anger, the times, collapse,
frustration and the fierce will to survive is
threatening now to replace our cool, tech-
nologized and violent apathy with risky passion
that is capable of, even, extremism in the pursuit of virtue, as Barry said, meaning something
else. There is convergence in our lives. We are
being called by the world to stand on our own
two feet at the very moment we are ready, perhaps for the first time, to do so.

This has happened to us already in negative
ways. The single most stimulating challenge to
our creative and not necessarily moderate
powers of imagination, caring and passion for
life is coming from our widespread experience
of collapse. The institutions we cherished once
are either crumbling around us or thoroughly
discredited. Old loyalties fade. The justice of
judges is questioned. Authority clings to its dignity like a pair of falling trousers. It succeeds
only in looking ridiculous. We are embarrassed
to show respect to superiors and even to each
other. Obligations which insure the survival of
families and communities have become intolera-
ble burdens. Wives walk out on their families

before their husbands have the chance that male supremacy used to guarantee them. The wealthy classes are seen more and more as exploiters, and it is commonly believed, as Tolstoy said, that behind every great fortune there is a crime. Priests are seen to be too preoccupied with their personal problems to pray for the people or with them. Anyone who occupies what was once a position of prestige is suspect. Teachers talk desperately of learning from their students while students cut class because they learn nothing from their teachers. Government "of the people" chokes in paper while governors complain that the faceless bureaucrats hold the power. Neighbors do not know each other's names. Gun sales are at an all time high. Most people feel far removed from the centers of power, which, like Atlantis, sank below the surface of the tumult. Who's in charge here, anyway? No one has a garbage man they can trust. The phones listen. Everyone wonders what happened.

What do human beings do in a situation like this? Well, they decide, perhaps, that their community, which is crumbling, is worth saving, since it is people. And then they set about to save it. They seek and create a new basis of community which will be the gathering all at once of political, economic, sociological, religious, personal, psychological and moral stresses into new patterns of sense. It is at that point of seeking and creating new communion and new language that we find ourselves now. This is what the rhetoric brokers mean by their tired word *revolution.* The first condition of "massive social mutation," to use Denis Goulet's phrase, has occurred. All that remains when the past passes is the future, which, unlike Billy's pilgrimage, will take its names from ours.

The new basis for community which we seek is justice. That proposition bores us and startles us both. It bores us with its triteness; what the hell is *justice* anyway? It is a word which, like the obscenities we cut in the brown desks of school days, is cut in marble up and down Pennsylvania Avenue and forgotten. It is one of the abstractions which we do not so much *speak* anymore as *yawn.* Justice, oh yes.

But we are startled, too. Justice! Do you hear? Justice now! The world screams it at us. Black people, old people, women, taxpayers, consumers, columnists, students, Chileans, nuns. Justice, dammit! We are startled by the instinct that in the midst of collapse, conversion seems possible. Conversion to a world of sharing and of ease between people who are different. We will never look at our world the way we once did. Or at ourselves. Justice is possible! It is the new basis of our common effort to live the one life of this frail planet together.

For some of us this dual experience of collapse and conversion takes the form of the dual discovery anew of *religion* and *resistance.* Two more words from the junkheap which we will brush off and use once more because their successors elude us. Religion and resistance, activities not of moderation but of desperation. It is our fierce will to survive which makes us pray, which makes us protest. Religion and resistance have come to mean the same thing. They have become our one way to "show an affirming flame."

Religion is not the same thing as the Church. Resistance is not the same thing as the movement against the American war in Asia. In fact, in an age which knows the dismantling of the Church we need ways in which to be *religious* more than ever; in a time when the war in Asia falls bloodily away like some terrified soldier being kicked from the rising skids of fleeing helicopters, we need ways to resist the systems of politics, economy and ideology that create in secret even now the next Vietnam. Religion is not finished when one form of the Church is, nor is resistance over when one horrible phase of the American war against the world is.

The collapse of the Church we knew and trusted once can be a *conversion* to religion which enshrines its faith in justice instead of finance because the abuse which made religion a device for social order and control of people's freedom is being exposed and discredited. Many of our early memories of oppressive power and authoritarian control have to do with religion and reveal to us its complicity in the massive contemporary assault on freedom. The arsenals of fire and fear which were available to our parents included all God's weapons and the threat of hell and immense reservoirs of guilt, in which, like bad pilgrims, we were dunked for our sins. We were housebroken by all those stories of disobedience and its dread consequences. Adam and, before him, the wicked angels were not good citizens. We knew early what trouble waited for bad boys and girls. There was only one law and it was only one word: "Obey!" Obey anything and everything, especially Mom, Dad, Sister Mary and Monsignor Stevens. Obedience was our first word for fear. Fear was our only word for God.

It was not long in our growing up before the domesticating effects of such stress on obedience was extended to the state. We understood the easy partnership Church leaders shared with the power brokers of politics and commerce. The religious ideology served the commerce of bishops and mayors and presidents and priests and bankers. The subtly interlocking alliance of authorities, all of whom had as much claim on our freedom as did God, left us all bowed, mumbling, quiet. Life was simple; it was, in sum, obedience. There was no alternative but going by the hand through bad-boy land.

One day the alliance of the gods broke. Whom do you obey when your authorities speak with conflicting voices? Whom do you obey when the gods argue or fall silent? It is at that moment that grace strikes. Grace is the revelation that none of the gods are God. At that moment you do what the Jews did; you stand up in your slavery and walk out of it. The religion of Israel and of Jesus is not the worship of subservience; it is the art of resistance. The collapse of "obedience" can be the condition of our conversion again to freedom and its Lord.

Israel was a community of protest against prevailing cultural idolatries. The Jews were (and still are in some ways) a fierce counter-culture.

They defined sin as the surrender of freedom. The ten commandments, which catalogue the ways people commonly went back to Egypt, were a celebration of freedom—not the orgy before the guilt-idol that we made of them. The basis for the community of this religious people was justice. Religion for them was an act of resistance against neighboring peoples who enslaved those who were different ("Thou shalt not steal *people*" is the way the fifth commandment read for the Jews); who cast aside the useless and unproductive members of society ("Thou shalt honor the old," whether they are still productive or not); who exploited women as sex objects ("Thou shalt not make an idol of sex"); who were enslaved to a work ethic that put property and production before persons ("Thou shalt not work always": take it easy on play-day).

For the Jews, justice was not a function of religion or even its consequence. Justice was religion itself. The Lord was known chiefly in his *justice*. Israel's story is the story of a people whose struggle was not to obey an external authority but to respond to their own conscientious impulse, as articulated especially by the prophets, toward social justice.

Every Jew was called to be "a just one." In Hebrew, the word *just* implies the attitude of the Lord which guarantees to all people uncritical favorable regard; the Lord's promise to his people depends on nothing of theirs—not their work, nor their holiness, nor their faithfulness.

The Lord is the faithful one. The *just* share in this *justice* of the Lord.

The Hebrew use of the word *just* involved a pun, which is why the one Hebrew word is translated also as "uprightness" or "righteousness." Justice is the act, literally, of standing upright. The just one stands on his own two feet. The image of standing had its origin in the liberation moment of deliverance from Egypt — which was the great experience for Israel of collapse *and* conversion. The Passover meal had to be eaten standing up, upright, "justly," because the people had to be ready to move out of the land of slavery at a moment's notice. No one knew when the great and horrible moment would come, but the *just* were ready.

Justice is the act of standing, ready to move out of one's present into the future. No commitment to political systems, economies, families, religions or neighborhoods can come in the way of such readiness. The just one's obedience consists in readiness to disobey Pharaoh. Whenever the people of Israel stopped standing ready, when they absolutized security or put property above persons, even, as with the temple, in the name of religion, there was an Amos or an Elias or a Jeremiah whose obedience consisted in disobedience, and whose religious proclamation was the cry for justice. When the prophets and the charismatic rebels were ignored, the just judgment of the Lord took the final form of grace—exile, collapse, conversion. Babylon, even in its weeping, was where the people met God again. On the road, away from home and old habits the people learned to stand again and walk. We know the pattern well.

Collapse *and* conversion. Exile *and* homewardness. Death *and* life. One thinks of Jesus. The glib talk fades and one makes what must pass these days for prayer:

We will not love you, Christ,
until you are convict again,
criminal, dangerous man, guilty as death.
We have no use for your holiness.
Leave the Church with us.
Come to the people.
We need no Savior from you.
For redemption we go to the Green Stamp
    store
where we buy our bishops and our judges
when we need them.
Leave your good robes.
Leave your godhead and your sainthood
and your testaments and your rituals.
We don't want your grace
or your sacraments or your succession
or your easy belief.

We want you to be in trouble again
like we are, slightly crazy
and inconsiderate and self-centered
enough not to kill for Caesar.
Jesus Christ, climb your dark poles again
and find us watching, awake this time.

It is a prayer which we do not so much utter as, to use Paul's word, "groan." It is a prayer first heard by the dumb walls of prisons and lately by the deadly skies of Asia; we want you to be in trouble again like we are!

Jesus was known neither for his moderation nor for his obedience to illegitimate earthly authority. The only incident his followers remembered from the thirty-year silence of his private life was an act of disobedience. Jesus proclaimed with his life that obeying God implies disobeying human beings, beginning with Mary and ending with Caesar. One's freedom is appropriately surrendered to no tyrant, nor even to a good woman. It is on one's *own* feet that he is called to stand!

Unless we domesticate it with gold and red silk, the memory of Jesus *must* disturb us. It destroys the ease with which we divide human beings into criminals, troublemakers and delinquents on the one hand and bankers, bosses and good boys on the other. God was a criminal;

how have we explained that? From Paul to Bon-hoeffer we learn that Christian theology is more at home in jails than in the palaces of cardinals; how do prison chaplains preach that sermon? Religion is not the same thing as social order. Religion is not obedience. Indeed, when we call Jesus the new Adam we imply that he redeems disobedience. Jesus did not put control above conversion. He warned his hearers repeatedly that following him would lead to trouble, and sure enough it did.

The followers of Jesus were known neither for moderation nor for obedience. Christians were all outlaws once. The first myth of saint-hood was the myth of martyrdom; the Church's best men and women disobeyed the state. And died thereby.

When the moment of reconciliation between Caesar and Papa occurred, some Christians still had the instincts of outlaws. Blood stopped flowing by and large, but the radical impulse that led to martyrdom led in the new age to monkhood. The desert became an act of resis-tance. Followers of Jesus repudiated the mar-ketplace and affirmed the connection between religion and resistance despite the conspiracy of emperors and bishops to deny it. You knew all this before, and so did I. It is important, though, to remember now and then. Especially now, when there are good men and women in prisons and criminals in high places.

Examining our religious heritage we discover that it is richer than we thought and not nearly as tame as the guards would have us think. The astounding future invites us to recover, from our past images of resistance, modes and models of refusal to surrender to illegitimate authority. We must nurture the counter-culture courage that took the form before of monkhood. We must imitate the disavowal of privilege and affluence won and protected by violence that was spoken of before as mortification. We must seek out and create communities of resistance in the shadow of the charismatic rebels who founded orders of men and women, most of which were Church-broken long ago.

The communities we seek are gatherings of spirit. The spiritual life itself is resistance. We remember that politics, as Péguy said, begins in mysticism. We are not embarrassed to acknowledge that politics in our priority, for *politics* is the word we use to describe our communion in flesh; the fact that we are here together means we must do something about it besides wonder. But we must wonder too, for being here in flesh is fine when you consider the possibilities. Every night I lay me down and thank God I'm not an angel.

We are not embarrassed to acknowledge that spirituality is our priority, for the thing about our flesh is its spirit. We are spiritually enfleshed. Each of us is an act in himself of communion. In our culture which seeks in thousands of ways to divide, polarize, dichotomize, discontinue, or, as the Army says in its bloody Latin, *interdict,* the commitment to sustain communion between flesh and spirit, between religion and politics, between "Yanks" and "Gooks," is itself an act of resistance.

Spirituality is the capacity human beings have to live in touch with the connections between things. The wind through these pine trees where I sit reveals it to us. The wind moves the trees. The trees move the birds. The birds move the bees. The bees move the flowers. The flowers move me. Instead of picking them I spare them for someone I love. Everything is connected to everything else. That is the point and it is difficult. It is spirit and, as the frog says about being green, not easy.

Spirituality is the commitment to the nurture of connections. It is precisely to this mingling of elements and decisions and loves which is holy communion that we were called by a Vietnamese poet who wrote to Americans on the occasion of Ho Chi Minh's death:

> Yes, because to make revolution you need
>   men,
> men with consciousness. So ask yourselves
>   first:
> what is consciousness without conscience,
> if not sterile intelligence?
> And what is conscience without generosity,
> if not just remorse and self-pity?
> And what is generosity without passion
> if not mere charity?
> And what is passion without an ideology
> if not only a dream?
> And what is an ideology without a vision
> if not a nightmare?

To be a spiritual person today is to believe that humanity is still possible. The humanity which is the mingling of consciousness, conscience, generosity, passion, ideas, dreams, vision. "Man is possible," this poet says, not from lofty fashion but from a bunker. The humanity we seek is a project on which we work and for which we pray together. The communion we celebrate and seek as our first priority is larger than we are—and more lively than all of us together. "Even if I die," the Vietnamese poet wrote before he died, "it will not end at dawn."

We give such primacy to communion because we know, and this is what makes us religious, human communion is more than human. The one life we share with Vietcong soldiers and "them good old boys" of Mississippi and the cane cutters of Cuba is the one life we share with God. Our other word for it is *grace*. And for now the only word we should allow for the one life of partnership among all of us including God is *justice*, for *justice* is the shared task by which we make this communion mean something to the very flesh of men and women. There is no room here for piety or glib talk, both of which are killing members of our one life, which is to say *people*. There is room for trembling; we "tremble for our country," as Thomas Jefferson said, thinking of slavery, when we "remember that God is just." We think of slavery and more and pray for the *gift* of that justice before it comes to us as vengeance.

When we hear the cry of our times for justice, and when we answer it by standing on our own two feet, exposed, ready, vulnerable to each other and to the future, we know what it is to be in exile. We are in exile from comfort, from easy consciences, from safety. We have left the trenches where we hid, partly of our own courage, partly because we were dragged out by

God's clinging faithfulness.

Jim Forest sees in the story of Kitty Genovese a metaphor of our time. You remember her, don't you? She was the young woman who was going home from work to her apartment in the Kew Gardens section of New York City. It was 1958 or 59. She was suddenly and brutally attacked by a mindless knife-wielder. Though she was stabbed, her screams frightened the man off, but he returned quickly when it was clear that no one was coming to her aid. Repeatedly, he attacked and was frightened away by her screams. And, repeatedly, he returned to stab her again when no one came to help. The police reported later that during the forty-five minute struggle in which Kitty Genovese screamed for help, about fifty people in a nearby apartment watched, listened, waited and did nothing. No one even called the police. Kitty Genovese was murdered by fifty people, one of whom used a knife. The others killed her with their cool detachment.

When we first heard the story of Kitty Genovese, we thought it was a story about New York City. It took the brutal and heartbreaking sixties to teach us that it is a story about us. *We* are the *ones* who live in the automated apartment building, protected and insulated and deaf to the cries of the victims who are in death-struggles just there beyond the ledges of our windows. We are protected from their screams by our music, by our witty conversation, by our bad poetry, by our air conditioning, by our paid police who keep strangers away from us. Most of our energy and nearly all our money (seventy-five percent at last report) goes toward protection. We protect ourselves with weapons and deodorant and contraceptives and seatbelts. We are the people who huddle together, yet alone, in the very middle of the Pentagon, the symbol of protection and of our people now. We will not leave, vulnerable, for anything. We are not New York. We are America. Kitty's story has become our own.

But there is another story. Another metaphor. Another name. Do you remember Hugh Mullin? No? His story was widely reported in August of 1971. The violence in Northern Ireland was in its seventh black blossoming and the story of Hugh Mullin, the shot priest, caught the tragedy of a whole people and yet the hope of a whole age.

A young Belfast workingman, Catholic, was returning home of an afternoon when he was cut down by British guns in one of those increasingly common and seemingly "unintended" incidents of death. Now it was Father Mullin's bad luck that the young man fell, bleeding, right in front of his rectory. A rectory is, after the Pentagon, the most protected place in the world. But no priest, however Irish, could ignore a fallen brother on his very doorstep. And so it was that Fr. Hugh Mullin left his novel or his football game or his siesta, left the insulation of his rectory to run into the street with oils, with his purple stole flapping in the wind. He bent over the wounded man, and while he was mumbling the last rites over the fallen workman, a second shot rang out from England. The priest slumped in sacred gesture, falling himself over the man he was anointing, dead. One thinks of Jesus, who responded to death by dying. One thinks of words he would like to say to Father Mullin:

> Did you know
> the last rites for O'Malley
> would be the last rites for you?
> As if the sacraments
> of death you bore—
> your black, your oil,
> your purple band,
> your crepe hovering—
> turned for once
> against you.
> You never knew the priesthood
> would be dangerous.

You learned after all
the only words death
knows of life: I die.
You were spared your own piety;
you just did it
in the middle of murmurs.
If I were the sun
watching you bless, bleeding,
I would have shrunk
into a candle doing vigil
in the corner of your church.
As it is small flames
casting shadows watch from
the corner of my eye.

Those of us who are believers still, believing
for our own sakes and not for our parents' or
our children's, are discovering that the easy ges-
tures of belief are losing their exemptions from
real life and their insulations from the cries of
victims. The collapse of the Catholic culture
and of our certain dogmas of Church and nation reveals us to ourselves. We are exposed.
We can no longer hide behind sacraments or rituals or forms or formulations. The holy water
font, like Don Maclean's levy, is dry.

The Irish priest left the rectory. He left the
ritual or it was taken from him. He dropped the
oils. The stain of blood made its own stole on

the purple ribbon he wore around his neck. A death band. His last last rites. The world conspired with war and a passing workman to make Father Hugh Mullin respond to death by dying.

One thinks of Jesus. One falls silent. We are not Irish or bleeding. We have not been flushed out of our protection *that* way yet. Out of our Pentagons, out of our rectories, out of our convents, out of our nice families. But still, here we are in the middle of the street, bent over a broken body. It may be our own. We are waiting for the final noise, mumbling to ourselves and to each other.

To use another of Jim Forest's metaphors, we have been *conscripted* by God and our times; we are not at liberty to refuse this call. We are not free to ignore the cry of a single human being in distress. The cry that drafts us is of all humanity.

The act of being vulnerable has become the political response the world needs from us most. Vulnerability is the antidote to the idol of protection. Only when we are vulnerable will we be just; *standing up* is like that—especially when you are standing in the streets of a war you did not start and cannot stop. The act of being vulnerable, personally, physically, spiritually, is the most profoundly political act available to us.

Disarmament: a politics of vulnerability. *Vulnerability:* a new basis for community. The community we seek with each other and with the world depends utterly on the individual and corporate decision to lay down arms—beginning with deodorant and ending with bombs.

The Church must disarm. It is folly to suppose religious people have *anything* to say to world leaders unless they themselves abandon their preoccupation with survival and protection. Rectories, convents, chanceries, bishops' houses, the Vatican—they are like outhouses to the Pentagon. The Church must come willingly out into the streets—with its people.

Justice, vulnerability, concern: we seek a community of justice, a politics of vulnerability and a religion of concern. It is all possible to us now. We have been dragged off into exile again—exile from comfort, ease and protection. We can hope yet to be at home in exile because we learn what our fathers and mothers in faith learned repeatedly: it is the Lord who calls us out of Egypt. What we thought was home was slavery. It is the Lord who sends us on this journey and he is with us in this exile, in these streets.

One thinks of Job who discovered his true wealth when he had lost everything. One thinks of Dr. King who responded to death by dying.

One thinks of Kitty Genovese. One thinks of
Hugh Mullin. He anointed the fallen with his
blood and was so anointed in return. This new
sacrament is the world's old one: blood broth-
erhood, sisterhood, One thinks of Jesus. One
falls silent.

9
Poetry and Other
Hints of God

A reflection of the religious uses of imagination must begin with a story. And it must be a story passed on by Elie Wiesel, taken originally from the Jewish stories of the Hasidic masters.

There was once an old rabbi whose wisdom and knowledge of the ways of mystery made him the leader of his people, Israel. Whenever the people were threatened with a catastrophe of whatever kind, they went to him with their plea: "Intercede for us with God to have him spare us again!"

At that the old rabbi would go into the heart of a dark and magic forest that only he knew of. Once in the sacred place, he would build a special magic fire that only he knew how to build. And once it was burning the old rabbi would say the words of a sacred prayer that only he knew. Then he would say to God:

"God, I am here in this dark place of mystery, before this magic fire, having said the sacred prayer that you might spare the people." And, always, God did spare the people.

The old rabbi died. When next the people Israel was threatened with catastrophe, they went to his chief disciple and asked him to intercede for them with God. Whereupon he went into the dark place of mystery in the heart of the forest. Once there, he built the magic fire that only he knew how to build. And then he said to God, "God, I am here in this place of mystery before this magic fire that you might spare the people. I do not know the words of the sacred prayer, so my being here in this holy place before this magic fire will have to be enough." And it was. And God spared the people again.

Well *he* died. The next time Israel was threatened with catastrophe, they went to *his* chief disciple and asked him to intercede for them with God. He went into the dark forest to the special place of mystery, where he knelt and said, "God, here I am in this sacred place that you might spare the people. I know neither how to build the magic fire nor the words of the secret prayer. So my being here in this holy place will have to be enough." And it was. And God spared the people again.

Well *he* died. The next time Israel was threatened with catastrophe, they went to *his* chief
disciple and asked him to intercede for them
with God. Well, he leaned back in the easy
chair of his living room, resting his head upon
his fist. He said, "God, I do not know how to
build the magic fire. I do not know the words of
the sacred prayer. I do not even know how to
find the holy place in the forest. So my telling
you this story will have to be enough." And it
was. And God spared the people again, because,
you see, God created human beings because he
loves stories.

It is our privilege and our terror to live in a
time when there is nothing left but stories. The
fires around which we gathered for light,
warmth and fellowship are dark now. The passion that held us together and that made us
young is cool now. The sacred places that as-
sured us of significance and guaranteed communion with the gods and with each other come
down to us as museums. We visit them faintly
curious, reminiscing and, finally, unaffected.
The sacred words that promised control to us of
our futures and even of God's slipped away like
old phone numbers set aside and then forgotten.
We can take neither communion nor communication for granted anymore.

When we gather, especially with our own kind, we find ourselves telling stories in ways we never did before. We are not used to looking back like this, but some common instinct toward gentleness prompts us each to tell the story we share. And so our talk turns toward the memories that make us a people. Did you listen under covers to the radio Lone Ranger? What were you doing the day John Kennedy died? And Martin? See this scar—Brother Andrew hit me with his monk's belt.

We live in a time when we are *aware* of the stories we tell. We are learning that human beings love each other and pass the time chiefly with their stories. *Story,* as Tolkien calls our very attitude toward life, is the basis of community. We are all engaged in the continual process of telling our *own* stories and making them the same as the story of our people. Loneliness dissolves in the discovery that one's story can never be told adequately unless someone else's story is told as well. We are limited by our stories as well as told by them. And those of us who claim to be believers make the preposterous claim that God's story will never be fully told until ours are. My story is not only yours. It is God's. And God's, when I claim it, is mine. He made us, you see, because he loves stories.

And so when we are inclined to celebrate or

mourn what happened to us, we say what it was. Stories enable us to name the past, to put a word on it, to claim it, bad and good, as our own. Even the dullest of us, even the least Irish of us, is able to be transformed into a storyteller when we find ourselves at a wake or a wedding.

When we anticipate the future, out of nervousness or happiness, we make it present by telling its stories too, even before they happen. We welcome the future or flee it by means of our fantasies and dreams and wishes, our memories of tomorrow, our stories which are begun but not ended. In this way we resist the fatalism that regards the future as something that happens to us; the storyteller claims, in fact, that *he* happens to the future. If you regard your life as a story *you* are telling, although in cooperation with others, then the future is not the enemy our times make of it, but the stuff out of which you tell yourself to yourself and to others.

To tell a story, whether of past in the form of memory or of the future in the form of dream, is to assert *power*. Storytelling is a human being's way of asserting himself personally, and, finally, politically. This is why the most powerful people in any community are its storytellers, its myth-makers. They are the ones who provide the images and the words other people use to tell their own tales. "The adjustment of man to

his environment," according to Walter Lipp-
mann, "takes place through the medium of fic-
tions." Storytellers create them. Revolution is
not so much a change in one's environment as a
change in the stories told about it.

The stories of our days tell about a crucial
and remarkable conversion that is occurring.
We are, I believe, being converted to a story-
way of life in which we are able to love what is
useless, as stories do.

As Kurt Vonnegut says, the key problem of
our age is "how to love people who have no
use." One need not go farther than Vonnegut
himself to discover what all storytellers know—
people are lovable because they are, not because
they are useful. Everyone has a story and therefore a right to interest, time, love and careful
listening. "There are eight million stories in the
Naked City," they used to say on television.
"This has been one of them."

The Hasidic tale we began with proclaims the
good news that, as far as God is concerned, the
feeblest story is worth more than all the magic
and all the prayers and all the tribute men pay
in their attempts to buy the gods. God's love for
his people does not depend—as they and we
thought—on the sacred place or the special fire
or the right words. God loves the story we are
telling with our lives, and he is as interested as

we are in seeing it to a proper conclusion.

Our discovery of ourselves as storytellers and the believing instinct that describes God as a storyteller—the "author of creation," as we used to say—reveal to us the centrality of imagination, the fragile vessel in human beings that brims over in stories. The imagination is the faculty which opens us to the divine; more important, it enables us to be human. An imaginative act by definition is an act of hope and gentleness. Imagination is the seat of prayer, which is why Kafka could claim that "all art is a form of prayer." It is the home of holiness. It is the way we have of being religious.

This is not to say imagination is not difficult, nor is it to say we do not imagine horrible and tragic realities. "Christ, you know," as John Lennon says, "it ain't easy." But we *imagine* precisely because much that we experience is painful, absurd, and discouraging enough to nearly break us. Imagination is what keeps us from breaking. William Lynch suggests in his book *Images of Hope* that a person will not despair as long as he can *imagine* a way out of his or her dilemma.

In my own life, the hopeful and healing effects of imagination are available mainly through the writing of poetry, my own peculiar form of storytelling. Like Mr. Santayana, I might presumptuously describe myself as "an ignorant man, almost a poet." A poem, when I make it, is the result of a process that begins with an experience which, because of its beauty, terror, pain or humor, I cannot understand, believe or claim as my own. What Wordsworth calls "intense emotion." Whether it is a bad event or a good one, the initial effect is that I am at its mercy. I am struck. I am seized, caught, passive. To be a human being is to know how to move from passivity to activity. When Genesis displays the first human beings as the namers of creation, the first poet of Scripture is describing the most basic way we have of asserting ourselves in the face of experience. If the world happens to us, it is also true that we happen to the world, and we do so chiefly by naming it. A human act. An act of power. An act of assertion. The word is the beginning of power. Control words and you control everything.

I have turned to my notebook at times out of deep gloom and depression. I have gone at such times in search of the word. I have tasted the despair that comes of collapsed meanings and ideas, say, of God or of ourselves. At moments like that, after weeping, after aimless hours in bed or walking, I have been moved to write the world down on paper—the world as it was mine. I have been moved at such times to make a poem. The act of poetry has been then the act of refusal to be dead or down. Imagination is its own healing. I have felt whole worlds lifted from my back by a few lousy little words on paper. We may call it only "getting it out." Wordsworth calls it "intense emotion recollected in tranquility." In gentleness. Imagination is our way of caring for ourselves when we need it most. It is tenderness in the old story of Elias: the fierce wind, the earthquake and the fire drive him only further into the cave in terror. Finally it is the gentle breeze, almost silent, that brings him out and speaks the word to him. What we all await are such *gentle* guides to God.

Samuel Coleridge defined imagination as the human faculty in which the "reconciliation of opposites" occurred. All the conflicting experiences of our existence, of what Coleridge calls our "warring nature," are transformed into images, into concrete movements, pictures, metaphors, symbols that seek out the inner unity that we believe holds all beings in being. Death and life, collapse and conversion, reason and emotion, detachment and involvement, guilt and apathy, and, ultimately, good and evil; the wonder is that such basic conflict does not destroy us but makes us interesting.

It is in order to cope with such oppositions that we tell stories, that we spin out fantasies, that we allow ourselves wishes, that we dare to dream, that we write poems. Laughter and compassion both spring from the moment of inner union, of coincidence, of oneness, of integrity that imagination makes available to us. There is no removal of the conflict, but a holding it in tension. Living with it. "Creative tension," we say glibly, meaning the difficult act of living somewhere between the womb and the tomb. We are half hung, half flying, between life and death. According to Allan Tate, "The meaning of poetry is its tension!" The same could be said of us. The root meaning of *tendere* in Latin is "to stretch." Living humanly is a matter of stretching, which is how we grow and why we groan. The trick is to stretch to the breaking point and then, not breaking, to stretch some more. Our meaning is in *our* tension.

In describing imagination as the "reconciliation of opposites," we can limit ourselves, as we have up to now, to a discussion of the sorts of polarities that plague us each privately, individually, alone. We all know that hidden and inner quest for harmony and integrity. But we cannot hear Coleridge's phrase, "warring nature," and think only of individual human beings. The times and what happens to our taxes won't let us be that narcissistic. We are at war with nearly the world, after all.

If imagination holds out to us the promise of *union* within ourselves, so too does it promise the possibility yet of cherished *communion* among all people. By acts of imagination, storytelling, ritual, poetry, we make real and concrete and detailed the massive one-life we share with God, each other and all people everywhere, the one-life which is denied and blasphemed whenever one person raises a fist in anger against another, much less drops bombs in cool detachment.

The imagination, because it seeks out unities and celebrates them, is always in some way involved in the struggle to renew the structures of the world. Indeed the gifts of imagination, so neglected in our days, are more necessary than ever if the revolution we seek is to be human and humane. As the art historian Bernard Berenson said, "All of the arts, poetry, music, ritual, the visible arts and theater must singly and together work to create the most comprehensive art of all—a humanized society and its masterpiece, free men."

When we are faithful to poetry we will be faithful to politics. Or, as Tate put it, "If poetry makes us more conscious of the complexity and meaning of our experience, it may have an eventual effect upon action, even political action." The poet, the seer, the dreamer, the imaginative ones are no more exempt from political responsibility than the priest is. Indeed, as in Yeat's great phrase, the poet is the one who must above all hold "reality and justice in a single thought." The imagination is the one human faculty which steadfastly refuses to accept the perennial human whine that reality and justice will never co-exist. "Be realistic," we are told by dull people whose lack of imagination is surpassed only by their disappointment when social systems *do* change for the better. We would like to claim as our own the imaginative and bold reply of the French student who scrawled on a Paris wall in 1968, "Be realistic; demand the impossible." If Vonnegut is right in saying that the key problem of our age is "how to love people who are no use," the imagination with its gifts of art and poetry is the key faculty. Imagination is the act of celebrating the useless. What good American father wants his daughter to marry a poet? Poets are hippies, some of whom get haircuts. They serve no "useful" or "productive" function in society. When they do, they stop being poets and become propagandists or ad writers.

In our culture we prize the "useful" use of words which we call communication, or, better, *communications.* Whole industries, from TV to shrinks, are dedicated to it. But we take rather for granted the "useless" use of words which we call *communion.* Communion is not holy anymore. The distinction is one I first discovered in Allan Tate who wrote, "We *use* communication: we *participate in* communion." Tate argued that we must distinguish the difference between mere communication and the rediscovery of the human condition in the living arts. When we communicate we may understand each other's meanings, but we do not thereby stand-under them, so to speak. We do not feel them as our own. We do not get inside the other's skin and look out, as Boo Radley said, through a stranger's eyes. It is the goal of our living to stand-under someone else's. That requires an act of imagination. "Men," Tate wrote, "in a dehumanized society may communicate but they cannot live in full communion." If you can't imagine, you can't commune; you can't identify in any full way with other people near or far. It is a condition we know well; indeed we have named this age of alienation for it.

A sign of the dehumanization of our society is the paucity of common images we have come to share. Our language and our attempts at imaginative expression have taken on the kind of plastic uniformity we have come to expect from Holiday Inns. Where once people interpreted themselves to each other by means of cultural myths and archetypal symbols which were enshrined in religious traditions and elaborate secular rituals, now we have in common whatever meager language television gives us. When I talk to a group of people about, say, the buffooneries of St. Peter or even of Falstaff I get the sort of polite attention people give you when you talk about something that is not theirs. But when I just so much as mention that contemporary buffoon who says "I can't believe I ate the *whole* thing," people react immediately, with the recognition that comes when you talk about what involves them directly. Alka Seltzer is a more significant source of common language and images in America today than either religious Scriptures or great literature. We hold in common commercials and little else. A major reason for this is that we are, I believe, losing hold of the art of reading, and the decay of modern society is nowhere more conspicuous than in that. Most students I know, for example, do not even read newspapers. I know myself how difficult it is to sustain a commitment to the simple act of reading regularly. There seem to be too many more important things to do, but of course there aren't. Just too many easier things. Maybe we should run ads on television that say "Reading: try it, you'll like it."

What makes all of this crucial is that imagination with its gifts of ritual, poetry, myth and story is the very basis of human community. When a group of people lose touch with their common imagination, they cannot long live in community together. It is the useless activity of art and ritual that makes us friends, as it was the time the Little Prince wasted on his rose that made it important to him.

Until we begin to enter imaginatively into the worlds, indeed into the skins, of other people, and especially of Third World people, the dream of human community will elude us. Our liberation will not occur until we take the liberation of oppressed peoples seriously and imaginatively enough to feel it as our own. The Vietnam war would have ended long before it did if Americans could only have identified imaginatively with Asian people, and bombed Asian people in particular. War policy in America is set as if machines were warring with other machines. War is flesh; Americans do not really believe that because we do not read Sean O'Casey, or Sophocles. We watch television, and television never touches us where we bleed. America's war against the world, of which Vietnam is only a phase, will end when we discover that we are brothers and sisters to all people. It will, I am afraid, take a magnificent act of imagination for that to happen. Or a catastrophe. Thinking of the Vietnamese, we might ask what George Bernard Shaw asked, thinking of St. Joan, "Must then a Christ perish in every age to save those who have no imagination?"

Imagination is our chief way of loving in ourselves and others what is useless. It is the source and the basis of the community we seek with each other. And, what is more, imagination is what makes it possible for us to be religious people.

According to Coleridge, "The imagination is the repetition in man of the creative 'I am' of God." When we create, when we draw order out of the chaos over which we hover, when we hold the opposites of our existence in some kind of reconciliation, we are alive with the very life of God. The unexpected accident in which, without fully intending it, we have imagined a new thing, told a new story, drawn new meaning out of our metaphors—that accident is what theologians call "grace." It is a moment of high joy, of affirmation, of more than myself, of more than the human. When the muse strikes we are pulled beyond ourselves and even beyond art. We are *beyond,* ready to give ourselves up again. "If there when grace dances," as Auden said, "I should dance."

Everything that we experience invites us to go beyond it into the realm of mystery, of wonder in which we discover ourselves to be religious again. Religion is the imaginative language with which we engage that realm where we are always slightly strangers. From this point of view, "everything is only a metaphor," as Norman O. Brown said; "there is only poetry." Imagination is the habit of seeing more than is before the eyes. As Teilhard says, "The whole of life lies in that verb—seeing."

In this context, the chief activity of religion, which is prayer, becomes not a particular practice that occurs at regular intervals through the day, but an inner tendency toward the inwardness of life which we name God. Prayer is not so much a matter of communication with God, to use Tate's distinction, as it is a matter of *communion* with him. God is not someone we *use*, whether to stop the war or win ball games; God is the one in whom we *participate* when we are most fully ourselves. We do so imaginatively in and with and through the metaphors of our existence—nature, experience, silence, solitude, memory, fear, and nothingness itself. In this way imagination itself becomes our chief metaphor for God; if you could imagine God imagining, you would be God and God would be you. God's act of imagination is what we call creation. Creation's act of imagination is humanity, and humanity's is mine.

I am a religious man. I am at home with my inability to understand God because I can stand-under God. I do so poetically. For me the chief poem of God is Jesus the carpenter. His poem, his story, which is the nexus of countless stories begun with Abraham and Sarah, discloses to me the hidden unities of my own story and its communion with yours and all people's. In Jesus I discover that my story and his story have become the same story, and it is God's, who made us after all because of his love for stories.

John Macquarrie, the Angelican theologian, describes Jesus in language that is remarkably similar to Coleridge's description of imagination. Jesus is, he says, "the balance of polarities." Jesus is the "point of reconciliation" between death and life, God and man, past and future. Jesus is *tension* made flesh. Or, as John's Gospel puts it, he is the Word. He is the poem. He is the story of God.

We are people who share a commitment and a call to keep that story alive. The Church is the place where the story of Jesus is told, where, as Scripture says, "the good news is proclaimed."

Belief is what happens when the story of Jesus and my story become experienced as inseparably the same. Church is *how* that happens and it is *what* happens when it does.

We tell the story of Jesus in a variety of ways. At the key moments of our lives we tell the story in the special, heightened poetry of sacraments. At times of birth, growth, maturity, decline and death we tell the simple story again, making it our own. A story of birth, death, water, desert, bread, wine, space, time. Religion with its art, ritual, poetry, theater is the act of imagination which celebrates and continues our insertion out of nothing into God. The power of the story we tell is the power of life over death.

Poetry may stand silent in the face of death — but not powerless. Imagination is the ability to create an alternative future to the grim emptiness that death seems to be. Because our powers of imagination are in decline today — you can look either at the state of the arts or of religion — we find it nearly impossible to deal directly and courageously with death. Death breaks the fragile tension to which we cling. We hide from it in our plastic rituals, behind our new puritanism which will tolerate any sort of pornography but no mention of the real death of someone we love. We hide from it behind the mourning-suited butlers whom we pay to sneak up the aisles during the last mumbled prayers and snatch the rich coffin from the dark church before we see it. Flaubert said that the artist, the soldier and the priest face death every day; so do we all. And it is our task to tend to the inner artists, soldiers and priests that live in each of us. Our inner artists and priests must conspire with an act of poetry which will be prayer to love death as it comes to us. Else the soldier that lives in each of us, afraid and seeking mercy, will hate death and hide from it or kill it again, as soldiers are always doing. It is only the repeated failure of our inner artfulness and our inner holiness to imagine our way through death to life that sets our inner harshness loose on the world.

Death is the last poem and it is ours to write. All our stories are practice for it. It begins like any poem with one word. A word of truthfulness and a word at once of vulnerability. Death is the ultimate disarmament. When it comes to us there is no hiding. Death is the moment imagination waits for; the moment to imagine life in the face of its denial; the moment to imagine, as religious people always have, the afterlife. And we do that not to anticipate our future but to transform our *present* experience. Even death is subject to the transformation that comes about through the special way of seeing that religious imagination is. "Seeing," Teilhard wrote, as we said before. "We might say the whole of life lies in that verb." And the whole of death.

It is this way of seeing that is part poetry and part foolishness that makes us religious people, people of faith. We take imagination seriously because it is the faculty which enables us to experience life and death as the metaphor of faith which we remember as a man. We accept the call to nurture this sacramental, sacral, sacred vision as our most precious heritage. Our way of looking at the world is our chief way of prayer. Our stories about it are acts of praise. The world *lives* with meaning for us and we celebrate it and we rejoice to claim that it is more than human. " 'Sister, speak to me of God,' " Kazanzakis said to the almond tree, "and the almond tree blossomed." In addition to loving stories, perhaps, God loves flowers. One thinks of Easter. One thinks of life when we thought it was death. One thinks of Jesus. One falls silent.

10
Prayer Is a Haunting

I went down to the sacred store
Where I'd heard the music years before
But the man there said the music wouldn't
    play.
In the streets the children screamed,
The lovers cried and the poets dreamed,
But not a word was spoken.
The church bells all were broken.

                                    Don Maclean

It is hard to know what's happening. We are
not religious, prayerful men and women in the
way that we once thought we were. Yet neither
are we quite irreligious or unspiritual. Hard,
clear, rigid meanings have been replaced for us
by vague instincts and subtle turnings toward
the inwardness of ourselves and other creatures.
It is an inwardness which, with some embar-

rassment perhaps, we name God. We feel like apologizing to our theologian friends for our simple, quiet, Quaker-like spirit. Their distinctions no longer interest us and we feel slightly guilty for our peace.

Our once clear-cut membership in what we thought of as the community of faith, the Church, has been replaced by an ill-defined sense of being somehow part of the Gospel story and the pilgrimage of those who seek to make it their own. Our own inner sense of being spiritual, while much less specified and directed, has intensified in some way we do not fully understand. We could claim even to live more closely in touch with our spiritual instinct than we ever did before. The church bells may be broken, but we are not.

For most of us, once easy to describe—and to follow—habits of prayer are gone. For the first time in our lives, we don't know how to pray. Indeed, we don't know how to use the word. When we enter a church now, we do not, as once we might have, splash our hand in water, kneel immediately and say three Hail Mary's. No, more subtly, we only alter our way of breathing, whether for God or for the musty air we do not know. We change our way of hearing, whether for God or for the silence we do not know. We alter slightly our way of seeing,

whether for God or for the darkness we do not
know. And all this happens to us not only in
church. When they asked him how to pray,
Thomas Merton said: "Pray? What's that? Pray
is how I breathe."

There is an old word that we use more and
more in explaining ourselves to each other. It is
"presence." Literally "pre-sense." Nothing specific, defined, rigid, spelled out. Nothing neat.
Nothing we possess or control. It is sensible,
but not quite sensible either. Nonsense, perhaps.
Indeed nonsense literally. It is an awareness we
have. A consciousness which regularly, but
especially in silence, tells us, almost warns us,
that there is more here than meets the eye. Or
the ear. Or one's breathing. We turn like plants
in morning toward the sun, knowing as little as
they about the strange source of light, warmth
and color which draws us. We know ourselves,
at times intensely, to be in a special kind of
presence. It is hard to know what other words
to use in speaking about it. We do know this
much: prayer is not what we thought it was.
And prayer involves being and activity outside
ourselves, in the way the dawn life of plants involves the sun. There is more here than us, and
prayer begins as a form of attention to the
vague presence that stirs at once within the
beyond. It is a subtle matter of altered breath-

ing and hearing and seeing. We linger at the image of a dawn flower and say, yes, it is something like blossoming. Like shifting petals. Quietly we flourish. We are a kind of morning glory.

We are in search of words with which to explain ourselves to ourselves. I am trying to explain myself to you. There is an image out of my past, and probably out of yours, which gathers into itself the intense knowledge of *presence* which alters breathing and seeing and hearing in the way which I am daring to call prayer. The image I am thinking of is the old, weathered, creaking haunted house of my childhood, and, I suspect, yours.

Call up the memory for a moment, the high weeds, the broken windows, the spider webs, the old well in the corner of the yard. The silence about the place. The awe, terror and delight you felt, crawling through the grass, closer, ever closer. Hardly breathing at all. Clutching the stone that, once close enough, you hurled with all your might at the top floor window, trying to smash the last bit of glass in the whole house. But you didn't wait to see if the stone hit home, for, turning, getting up, you ran, someone screaming that they heard it coming. It was then you felt clearly, clearly, without vagueness, the presence we have been talking about. It is the presence that makes us at once terrified, and delightfully playful.

You may remember Boo Radley, the name by which such a haunting presence went in Scott and Jeremy Finch's neighborhood in *To Kill a Mockingbird.* Boo's house down the street was the fixed point in their universe. Everything turned around his place, which they ran past every day on the way to and from school. They never saw Boo Radley but he was there; they could tell by the way their breathing changed as they drew near his house, and their hearing and their seeing. Children understand haunted houses, how to fear them and how to play with them. Children seem able to live with the kind of vague turning which transforms everything in the presence of haunted silence. In the presence—I hesitate to use the word—of a ghost.

There, I said it, *the ghost.* What I have been trying to say all this time is that I am haunted. I am pursued. There is an intense, fearful presence, nameless, disturbing; and it is just over my shoulder, always. It is what I run from. When I summon up my courage and stop, turn to face it, to have it out, to wrestle Jacob-like, the ghost is gone, not quite there. There is a ribbon of darkness around all my light.

Part of the experience of being haunted is not

knowing who or what it is that tugs from all our margins at our attention. I am haunted by what I know is gone, by dashed hopes and expectations. By all these "too many people who have died" blowing in the wind. Buddy Holly, Janis Joplin and the music which we lost when we lost them. We are haunted by the most compassionate leaders our nation could produce, dead now several years. Governor Wallace was shot one spring; our hearts stopped for a moment and I was taken back, touched again by the ghost of my innocence. I am haunted by the dead of the war, Vietnamese and American, and by the ghosts of Errol Flynn and Gary Cooper who taught us how to get our fast guns out of our holsters, but they never taught us how to put them back. I am haunted by the ghosts of my cherished idols, Church, country, styles of life which elude me or turn continually to ashes.

It is not, I gather, unusual for a person or a people who have suffered a shocking death, whether of a loved one or a loved way of life, to experience the strange presence beyond and within that we call ghosts. Scott and Jeremy Finch discovered their ghostly neighbor after they had lost their mother. If you think this talk of ghosts is mere superstition or childishness and therefore to be dismissed, you know too little both of death and poetry. The last great gasp of the once vast Indian civilization of the Americas was a short-lived but powerful movement of hope and reconciliation—but not passive submission to the final act of white murder —which the Indians knew as the dance of the ghosts. In the dying grass moon of 1870, when the Indians were a ghost themselves of what they had been only forty years before, before the white armies of the north and south turned their blood thirst west, the reservations, especially those of the Sioux nation, were swept by the dance religion of the ghosts. It was the redman's way of coming to terms with the presence that haunted them. And, as the Indians said, that great presence was partly of the slain ancestor and partly of the good spirit still living. White men, in their final act of cruelty, dismissed the Indian attempt to love the grim past and accept the uncertain future as "pernicious religion." If the Indians had turned in the end to killing instead of dancing, the whites would have understood. What Indians knew, what we learn slowly, is that the ghost can be a metaphor for the deepest enlightenment which results from some great shock—a shock which discloses the communion with all life, past and to come, which belongs to men when they accept it. It was Boo Radley, in the end, who saved the children and taught them how to love.

> And the three men I admired the most
> (The Father, Son, and Holy Ghost),
> They caught the last train to the coast
> The day the music died.

Beginning with the day the music died for the first friends of Jesus—it was a Friday; it was the day their music who was a man died—Christians have grappled with the ghost-metaphor to describe their experience of the way the Lord remains present as he promised. We have been ghost dancers from the beginning, in our own uninhibited ways. After the shock of the death of Jesus, after the initial experience of loss, expressed best by the melancholy understatement of the Emmaus-brother who said to the stranger: "We were hoping he would be the one," we are always just getting our disappointed hopes.

But the stranger turned out to be a ghost. He disappeared upon recognition as ghosts are wont to do. Soon all the brothers were alive again with stories of the life through death of Jesus. "Amazing" is the word they used to describe the ghost stories that gathered them as he had once gathered them himself. On the road. To the women. In the upper room. By the sea of Tiberias. On the hill in Galilee.

But it was not a ghost. It was Jesus himself, in the flesh. Luke tells of their discovery this way: "They were still talking about all this when he himself stood among them and said to them, 'Peace be with you!' In a state of alarm and fright, they thought they were seeing a ghost. But he said, 'Why are you so agitated, and why are there doubts rising in your hearts? Look at my hands and feet; yes, it is I indeed. Touch me and see for yourselves; a ghost has no flesh and bones as you can see I have!' and as he said this he showed them his hands and his feet. Their joy was so great that they still could not believe it, and they stood there dumbfounded; so he said to them, 'Have you anything here to eat?' And they offered him a piece of grilled fish which he took and ate before their eyes" (Lk. 24, 36-43).

Jesus, as it turned out, was not a ghost, though the experience of his presence in resurrection was ghostly. His friends were haunted by him, even after his last appearance, which we remember as his ascension.

How we shrink from the word *ghost*. We are frightened of it as if it were itself a haunted house on the hill. It strikes me as curious that during these years when the pushy, dull liturgists (among whom we count ourselves) forced us to put all of our Latin into English, they took the one good, earthy, scary, Anglo-Saxon word we had and made us put it into Latin. We once were comfortable in speaking of God as a ghost. "In the name of the Father, and of the Son, and of the Holy Ghost," we said without blushing. But now we call him "Spirit." Now, don't get me wrong: I *love* the word "Spirit." Its connotations of wind and breath which return us to magnificent Hebrew imagery disclosed new marvels of God to us. We welcomed the word "Spirit" and we took it to ourselves with great naturalness, overnight.

But there was also a magnificence, newly relevant, about the early Christian instinct to think of God as a ghost. It is an image we have lost, and sadly. Latin always seems to domesticate—housebreak—the Anglo-Saxon and deprive it of its earthy harshness and full force. God is like a ghost to us—which is more than wind and more than breath. "Ghosts" are fearsome in a way that "spirits" are not.

A ghost reminds us immediately of death and such reminders are not allowed these days. Death owns the taboo we once reserved for sex. A ghost, when it haunts you, is persistent and clings to your house or name long past the time of your choosing. God is like that. We call him faithful. A ghost, unlike a wind, is personal, in search of relationship. God is like that. A ghost is not subject to our control; indeed a ghost is often quite irrational by our standards. And so is God. A ghost is in exile from home and from rest, on the move, in search of peace. And God is like that too in his communion with our exile. We do not possess the ghost who haunts us; indeed, whenever we recognize his presence he disappears. Like God, who is never quite there, whose presence always implies a kind of absence, a kind of trailing off in mystery.

It took Don Maclean in his song "Bye, Bye, Miss American Pie" to remind us recently of the ease with which we used this strange metaphor for God before. And then we remembered Hopkins' line, the magnificent image of God which is as old as Genesis: "The Holy Ghost over the bent world broods with warm breast and, ah, bright wings." In the beginning the world was haunted, and so it remains. But the great affirmation we make about the ghost of God is that this ghost is holy. Trustworthy. His haunting consists in the seduction of life out of all our forms of death, of order and beauty out of all our forms of chaos. The ghost of God is the Holy Ghost, in whose name we pray.

Now we are ready to say one more word—Lord, have mercy on us—about prayer. Prayer is the act of being haunted by God. This is the shocking way of speaking about prayer that

Paul, the most shocking of men, had. Paul knew about ghosts, how they groan, moan, wail and rattle chains in communion with the underworld that waits to be set free from its slavery. He said, "The Ghost comes to help us in our weakness. When we cannot find words with which to pray properly, the Ghost himself expresses our plea with sighs and moans too deep for words. And God, who knows our hearts as his own, knows what the Ghost means. The moans of the saints expressed by the Ghost are according to the heart of God" (Rom. 8, 26-27).

God haunts your soul. His spirit and your spirit are united and they make together one common plea for the world. Prayer is simply our way of identifying the haunting depth of our own inwardness with the haunting God. Prayer accepts the state of being haunted as a kind of grace. Prayer listens to that Spirit who speaks the name we long to use of God, distant, unknown, undisclosed; the Spirit names him "Abba, Father." Prayer listens to the wind, and, like Elias in his cave, hears the voice of God in the gentle breeze. Prayer accepts the Ghost's identification with our exile and learns something new about God. Prayer accepts the Ghost's identification with our vulnerability and learns something new about human beings. Our very yearning for freedom and for meaning and for home is the way God is present to us as uncritical love. With a tenderness we do not expect from him, Paul says our hiddenmost sigh is God's breath within us. Because it is God's immense breathing, this sigh goes beyond us and brings us with it in the same moment.

The Church is where we make such sighs with other men and women. It is breath together, conspiracy. It is the gathering which hovers over chaos; such hovering, such brooding, is our common act of prayer. We make our prayer and we become "warm breast and, ah, bright wings" for each other.

Speaking in this way of God as our Ghost makes us grim and playful at the same time. It is a metaphor with its own sense of humor, inviting us to be children. Prayer for us is something like whistling down the wind, surging past the graveyard in the dead of night, ready to laugh or cry, to summon up the Ghost and flee it when it comes. We flee dancing. We are strange people, we haunted ones. We are what this world looks for in late movies or weird places. But, like our parents of Pentecost, we surprise and embarrass the world and go out in the morning to the marketplace. They think we are drunk or "pernicious" or fools and they are nearly right.

We are among those who cry in the wilderness. We devour the roots of the burning bush. We live in the shadow of the absolute and we know it. We are, with Leon Bloy, "trustees of vengeance and the very obedient servants of an alien fury." We have turned into fire. We are the fire that will not go out because, unlike Prometheus, we did not steal our flame. It fell on us, split tongues, scorching our hair, a gift from God. Indeed our fire is his very life in us. We will not be silent. We speak words, given us again by Leon Bloy: "An obedient son of the Church, I am nonetheless in communion of impatience with all the mutinous, all the disillusioned, all those who have cried and not been heard, all the damned of the world. When I remember this multitude a hand grasps me by the hair and carries me off, beyond the relative demands of a social order, into the absolute of a vision of injustice such as would bring tears to the pride of the world's philosophies. I know all the reasonable things that virtuous people can say to each other to console themselves for the temporal damnation of three-quarters of humanity. I, the newcomer, feel that a death agony of six thousand years perhaps gives me the right to be impatient as men have never been and, since we must lift up our hearts, the right to tear those despairing organs once and for all from our bosoms in order to stone heaven with them! Such is the *Sursum Corda* of all the abandoned in this ultimate century."

Lift up your hearts. We have lifted them up to the Lord. Let us give thanks to the Lord our God. It is right and just. We give thanks especially for the Church, which touches us with such communion with the true ghosts of our age, the devoured ones; for the Church which suckles within us this foreboding of the infinite. This refusal at once to be silent before the speechless and to speak what is unspeakable. We give thanks for what we detect within the margins of our *own* souls. What we thought was chaos in our religion, in our nation, has turned out to be his Ghost, haunting us with our own humility. What we thought was homesickness reveals itself as pilgrimage. What we thought was the end turns out to be the prologue of an unspeakable drama, the like of which has not been seen for twenty centuries. The times which are cruel and immensely beautiful invite us to recollection. We are plunged, down, spiraling to the center of being itself where we discover old words with which we address the silence, saying, "Holy, holy, holy Lord, God of power and might. Heaven and earth are filled with your glory. Hosannah! Blessed is the desert traveler, and blessed are the companions he seeks. Blessed are we when we enter the black immen-

sity you are to us, leaving our hearts before us
like great torches." And we are singing:

> Bye, bye, Miss American Pie.
> Drove my Chevy to the levy but the levy
>   was dry
> And them good old boys were drinking
>   whiskey and rye
> Singin', "This'll be the day that I die.
> This'll be the day that I die."

When we confront ourselves in that way, in
our contingency, in our deathfulness, we are
very close to nothing, to nothingness, to
"nada." We are very close to prayer. We are
very close to the way in which we haunt ourselves. Prayer comes to maturity in us at the
moment when we confront our own ghost. It
may begin long before the day that we die, but
when it begins that dread day has begun too.
We hear ourselves described in this by Albert
Camus: "During every day of an unillustrious
life time carries us. But a moment always
comes when we have to carry it. We live on the
future: 'Tomorrow,' 'Later on,' 'You will understand when you are old enough.' Such irrele-
vancies are wonderful, for after all it's a matter
of dying. Yet a day comes when a man notices
or says that he is thirty. He belongs to time,

and by the horror that seizes him, he recognizes his worst enemy. Tomorrow, he was longing for tomorrow, whereas everything in him ought to reject it. That revolt of the flesh is absurd."

So we come to the heart of the matter. All that I have been trying to say in this way about prayer is that I am twenty-nine years old. I am afraid of turning thirty. The future is as little subject to my control as is the past. The ghost with whom I try in my stumbling ways to dance and whom at the same time I try to flee lives behind me, but ahead of me too. The moment has come when I must carry time. There are ghosts of the past and there are ghosts of the future, but now I must haunt the earth, which is deadly in need of ghosts who have learned to love.

Prayer itself is such a ghost, breathing down on us from yesterday and tomorrow. Prayer is one of the absolutes toward which we are on pilgrimage. We do not possess it. We do not "do" it. We move toward it, half in its power. But prayer does not carry us. There comes a time when we must carry it, though it eludes us, though "we do not," as Paul says, "know how to put it into words." But words, though we usually think of them as first, are the last things that happen to prayer. The first thing that happens to prayer must be ourselves.

Turning thirty is how we happen to ourselves. Turning thirty, which can happen at any age, is a metaphor for enlightenment, which, curiously, seems almost always to involve the loss of light and the sudden divesting of illusions. What the world was surely going to be when you were twenty it never was. The intense assurance with which we threw ourselves into the future as if it were a midnight pool and we were naked is mainly embarrassing now. It is daylight and we are still without clothes. Not only is the world a harsher place than we thought, but so are we. Yet it is all we have, as we are all it has; having failed in our grand efforts to see the world the way we wanted it, it is time for us to see it the way it is. Having failed to manipulate beauty, it is time to reverence it. Having failed to tech- nologize prayer, it is time simply to live in its shadow. We assert our youthfulness by leaving it behind.

We do not leave behind us the passionate conflict by which we measure God; our struggle has just begun. We must deal continuously with the further haunting of our enlightenment. Ma- turity, whether in love or prayer, comes at such a price because it has its own difficulties. I will not go gently into thirty, much less into the final night. I am fighting and kicking to stay alive. "With the awakening," Camus says, "comes in time the consequence: suicide or recovery."

Do not think that prayer is not dangerous; it leads to the consciousness of freedom with which everything begins. It faces us with what we would like to remain hidden; every choice we make is a choice for death or life. And we are choosing both all the time. Suicide or recovery; harsh words. Melodramatic. But true. If you can dare to touch the way you are dying of life now, in secret, you can pray. Prayer, remember, in us is like the subtle turning of morning's plant life to the sun. The turning I call prayer comes not of curiosity. Not of duty, not of habit, not of technique, but of necessity. Of desperation. Of yearning. We are in the grip of the inhuman, of darkness, of night. I am dying. You are dying. It is the feeling we share — prayer; we need to be redeemed.

If you can dare to touch the way you are dying of life now, in secret, you can pray. You can say: *Lord, have mercy. Christ, have mercy. Lord, have mercy on me.*

It was enlightenment, awakening and turning thirty that taught Jesus how to pray. Ghosts of his youth and the old age he would not have haunted him. He knew what prayer was, what we have been trying to understand, standing under this shadow of his last night. It was the night he was with his friends. It was the night in which he knew he was betrayed not by one man but by the whole of his life. He was not singing. It was a time for praying but not for words.

It was time to pray because God was gone. God *is* gone. God is gone; it is therefore time to pray. Maybe this is growing up or maybe this is dying. God is gone, or he would tell us. It is a time for praying but not for words. And so, since it is night, we take bread and break it and eat it and it is our body. And we take wine and pass it and drink and it is our blood. We have bled together, we have risen. We are doing this to remember who we are, because we forget. We are doing this because our only prayer has become an act of waiting.

> While I waited
> mountains seemed to move.
> Stones shifted.
> Air held itself.
> I heard great breaths.
> "Behold the one," I murmured.
> "Behold, he comes," I said,
> turning with shudders.
> But it was not God.
> It was you.
> It was you.

We find ourselves at communion—literally. That is where we do what finding we can. I eat you. I drink you. Prayer for us is that obscene and that physical. We cannot separate prayer from the flesh, from the blood of who we are. *That* is what I have been trying to say. We believe in the primacy of communion. And this communion is a metaphor of all forms of human love. It is a moment of marching, of hands awkward in their refusal to be pious. We will not fold them. Eyes closed. Kneeling. Tongues out, the taste, the anticlimax. We remember the first time, our white dresses and suits with long pants. It is a memory of ghost. The ghosts we were to each other then, the ghosts we have become. Because the Ghost of God is holy, the communion we share is holy too. It is communion with the fallen grain of wheat and the crushed grape and with God.

> When I turned again
> without trembling
> it was not you.
> It was God
> It was God.

Having drunk each other and eaten his words, we prepare to leave. We are leaving the place where prayers go when they want to pray.

We leave with blessings, having blessed each other, having spoken the names we yearned to hear again, our very own, and having been speechless in the name of the Father, the Son and the Holy Ghost. The three names we understand the least, Amen. We put away the priest but not the prayer. *Ite, Missa est.* Ghostly sound. *Deo Gratias.* God's grace. One thinks of saying thank you. But all the words are said. One thinks again, in the end as in the beginning, of Jesus. One falls silent.

III

A Tale

11
The Tinker King

It was a cricket. It was stuck on a thorn where
it landed in its last long jump. It was dead.

The old tinker was very careful as he picked
the poor cricket up and wrapped it in a leaf. He
put it in the pocket of his tattered vest, shaking
his head sadly. He would give the small creature
a proper burial in a field he knew farther down
the road. The old tinker was a man who knew
that he died a little whenever anything died a
lot. He saw connections. He was a gentle man
with death. And with life.

He always was, they said, whispering their
strange stories about him. Some men claimed,
half laughing, the old tinker had been a king
once, the king indeed of the very realm through
which he wandered now as a tinsmith, knife-
sharpener, pot-fixer.

It was true that in times past the realm had

lost its king and had been ruled for years now by the cohort of knights who were very cruel. It was true that in times past the king had lost the jewel of rule, which was the mysterious source of royal power. When the jewel of rule was gone, all the people knew it without being told, and the king had had no choice but to leave his throne. It was sad because the young king had been a good man, much better than the cruel knights, but without the great jewel of rule, the king could not be king. He could not dispense decisive wisdom and powerful guidance as kings must if they are not to be chased away by their very own cohort of knights. Though the people did not know how or why, their young king had lost the jewel of rule in times past.

The stories about the old tinker said it happened this way. The young king was a dreaming man, and that is always dangerous in a king. He was a man who asked many questions, who saw connections and who, all in all, was much too foolish to be king. Or altogether much too wise.

For example, it was said that on the day of his coronation, when they brought him his magnificent ermine robe, the young king asked where it came from. The courtier replied that it came from the royal merchant, to which the king replied with the same question: "But where did it come from?" The courtier then replied that it came from Persia or some such place, but the king was not satisfied and asked his question again and again until the courtier said, "Majesty, your fine robe comes from the small animals whom the hunters trap." When the courtier said that, the king was silent. He looked at the fine ermine robe. He touched it softly, sadly. He said, "Why should we wear such cruelty for a robe?" They put the ermine robe aside, bewildered by the king's questions. It was a beautiful royal garment. The young king refused to wear it.

Another time a visiting prince brought a gift to the king. It was a pearl of immense value. When the prince offered it to the king, he said, "Majesty, receive this pearl of great price as a sign of my homage." But the king asked the prince another of his questions: "Why is this pearl worth so much?" The prince replied smoothly, "Because of its perfect, moonlike shape." But the king asked again, "Why is it worth so much?" The prince hesitated and then said, "Because, Highness, it was so difficult to retrieve from the ocean's floor." But the king asked again, "Why is it worth so much?" The prince replied, but the king kept asking until finally the prince said, "This pearl is valuable because sixteen male slaves drowned in their diving to retrieve it." When the prince said that, the king was silent. He looked at the perfect, moon-shaped pearl. He touched it softly, sadly. He said, "Why should we wear such cruelty for a jewel?" They put the pearl of great price aside, bewildered again by the king's questions. It was a beautiful gift. The king refused to accept it.

It was the sort of thing the court came to expect of the king. It was not his questions they found impossible, however, but his refusal to go beyond them. When they were exasperated by his cancellation of the seasonal feast because the food was taken as special tribute from the peasants, they asked him, "Well, what have we to do with the lives of those who toil for us?" He replied only with the same question: "Yes, what *have* we to do with the lives of those who toil for us?" Soon the king had refused all the rights and trappings of his high office, but he replaced them only with confusion. He may have seen connections before and better than others, but he was only rendered powerless by what he saw. He took no steps to change the customs of the kingdom. He did not give away the wealth of the castle, for example, but was only saddened by it. He was a gentle man. And soon all the people thought he was too gentle, in his questions, to be king. He had lost the jewel of rule.

That is why, they said in their stories, the king left his throne and learned the wandering trade of tinsmithing and knife-sharpening. He could travel wherever he chose, seeing connections, asking questions, bearing the sad weight of the world's many cruelties and having to do nothing about them. Tinkers are free to be melancholy wise men as kings are not. They said the young king became the old tinker so that he could wander the kingdom in search of the jewel of rule, or in flight from it. Searching for and fleeing from long ago became the same thing for the dreaming old man in his wandering.

As he moved through the towns and villages, the tinker got to know and care for the common people of the kingdom. He entered their small houses by the back doors. He sat in their warm kitchens with them, fixing their tin pots, sharpening their bread knives and listening to their answers to his questions. He asked them everything and they told him because he was a man who listened with his eyes.

The tinker saw connections. He saw that the people were very unhappy. The harder they worked, the more the ruling knights took from them. The roads were in disrepair. The bridges were falling down. The water was fouled. The kingdom was suffering from years and years of bad rule.

There was a man whose son died in the fields while working too hard, gathering the monthly tribute tax. When the tinker asked him, "Who has done this to your son?", the man replied, "The heat did it. The sun." But the tinker pressed him, "Who did this death to your boy?" Finally the man said it: "The knights did this! The knights have killed my boy!"

The people who were standing near murmured. Such talk out loud was dangerous in the streets. As the truth always was. The dead boy's father asked the tinker, "What are we to do?" But the tinker said nothing. He was sharpening the bread knife the boy's mother gave to him. "What are we to do?" the boy's father screamed at him. The tinker did not reply. The father was very angry at him. "You see connections. You make us see them with your questions. But, having seen, what are we to do?"

The tinker stared at the knife he was sharpening at his wheel. He held it up before his face, running his thumb along its edge. The tinker said slowly then, "The knights have not ruled this realm forever, nor will they."

"But they have big swords," the dead boy's father said. "We have only our farming tools, our kitchen knives." The tinker put the knife down.

"When the time comes," he said, "you will

need no edges, but only stout poles and the branches of trees." They did not understand what the old tinsmith meant by this. They would have laughed at him but for the old stories and for the new clear look in his eye as he spoke. From then on the people listened to his questions more carefully. More and more his asking was the same: "Why should we pay with our children's lives for the excessive pleasures of the few who rule us?" But more and more the answer was the same: "Because those who rule us have heavy swords, while we have none."

On the day this story began, remember, the old tinker was going down the road with a dead cricket in the pocket of his tattered vest. He came to the field he knew of, left the road and walked to its center. There he knelt and very carefully scooped out a handful of soft dirt. He took the cricket, wrapped it in its leaf, and was about to bury it when he was interrupted by a great huge knight, all in armor, riding a black stallion.

"What are you doing there, old fool?" the knight asked. "Who is asking?" the tinker replied, posing his own question, as he was wont to do. "I am one of the ruling knights! How dare you speak to me so?" With that the knight kicked the old tinker swiftly.

The knight pointed to the battered tinker-cart that was still in the road. "Is that your cart and whet wheel back there?"

"It is," the old man said, asking no more questions. "Well, up then," the knight said. "You're coming with me!"

The big knight made the tinker follow him, pushing his cart as fast as he could. They were going, they both knew without saying, to the royal castle. When they finally arrived, the knight told the tinker to wait in the corner of the courtyard, and then he went off yelling, "Brothers, Noble knights. Behold! Behold! I've brought a tinker to sharpen our weapons. Bring your swords and axes! A tinker to put fine edges on all our steel!"

And so it was that the ruling knights brought their swords and axes and knives and lances to the old tinker, who did as he was told. He began putting fine edges on the weapons of the cruel rulers. He was bent over his turning wheel, it seemed, forever. And sharpen he did. When the knights returned for their swords they were very pleased, for the edges surely were the sharpest any had ever seen. Sharp enough to cut fine paper. The knights were so pleased, in fact, that they did not cut the old tinker's head off but let him go instead.

When the tinker went to a nearby village, the people were surprised and glad to see him. They said, "What questions did they teach you this time, tinker?" They asked him this because, remember, he was always asking questions of them.

But now he said, "The time is here! Gather your stout poles! Spread the word!" Because he spoke as if it were the truth, the people did as he said. Soon the villages and towns of the whole realm had heard that the old tinker was not asking anymore, but telling. He was telling the time. "The time is here," the people whispered to each other.

At dawn one morning all the people of the realm gathered in the great plain outside the castle where the cruel ruling knights lived. They gathered—men, women and children—each with his stout pole or kitchen tool or branches of trees. They were all ready. In front of them, nearest the castle, stood the old tinker.

Then the great wooden door of the castle wall creaked open and the crowd of mounted knights appeared. Their armor and weapons glistened in the morning light, shining still from the burnishing and sharpening the old tinker had accomplished. The knights prepared to charge into the crowd of commonfolk who began to murmur, "We are no match with our poor sticks for such armed knights. Why are we here?"

At that the tinker climbed to the top of his battered cart, nearly falling as he did so. He hollered at the crowd his final question, "Why are you here?", and his first answer, "You are here because everything is connected to everything else!"

"But we are about to die!" the people shouted. To which the tinker replied, "You are about to live!" The knights began coming slowly out of the castle, ready to charge. When the tinker saw their readiness he hollered his final words at the crowd: "Do not strike these men, these cruel knights. They are your poorest sons. Only stop their swords with your sticks and you will see."

No one understood what the tinker meant, least of all the knights who began their charge, laughing, roaring. The big knight on the black stallion made for the tinker, his sword flashing above his head. As he was about to strike, the tinker held a frail branch over his head. The knight made as if to cut through the branch and kill the tinker. His sword slashed into the thin wood and then, instantly, remarkably, the flashing metal withered and curled in its cutting. The tinker, in sharpening the knights' weapons to such fine edges, had ground away their thickness, their substance, on his wheel. The weapons of all the knights were sharp to the eye and to the soft touch. But when swung to strike a blow, they withered like tissue. And the people saw. They held their sticks and branches high, as one by one the knights were disarmed. The weapons were honed much too finely. At every strike, every sword, axe and knife disintegrated. The people cheered.

It could hardly be called a battle. No one died that day. When the last knight was embarrassed in his disarmament, the crowd turned to the tinker. His eyes flashed clarity, dreaming and joy—a brilliant jewel. One of the older knights, looking at the tinker, said loudly, "I see in his eyes the jewel of rule which was lost, lo, these many years."

But the tinker said, "What you see is the flash of the common mirror every old man is privileged to be once before he dies. What you see in my eyes is the jewel of rule that belongs to you all." The people cheered him. They would have made him king, which he did not want, which by then they did not need. Their cheering was interrupted, though, when the old tinker, who was worn out at last, fell over and died.

Very carefully they picked him up, wrapped

him in a leaf and carried him to a field nearby. They carried him on his cart. All the people knew they died a little whenever anything died a lot. It was their new way of living. They saw connections. They were a gentle people with death and life.